DESCARTES
AND
HUME

Other Titles of Interest

BAUM, J. A.
Montesquieu and Social Theory

BUNGE, M.
The Mind-Body Problem

FITZGERALD, R.
The Sources of Hope

GEYER, F.
Alienation Theories: A General Systems Approach

KHOSHKISH, A.
The Socio-Political Complex

MACHADO, L.
The Right to be Intelligent

PECCEI, A.
The Human Quality

RICHARDS, T.
The Language of Reason

SCHAFF, A.
History and Truth

TALMOR, E.
Mind and Political Concepts

A Pergamon Journal of Related Interest

HISTORY OF EUROPEAN IDEAS*
Editor:
Dr. Ezra Talmor, *Haifa University, Israel*

History of European Ideas is a multidisciplinary journal
devoted to the study of the history of the cultural exchange between
European nations and the influence of this exchange on the formation
of European ideas and the emergence of the idea of Europe. The journal
publishes regular review articles as well as a book review section;
it also contains current information about European scholarly meetings
and publications.

Free specimen copies available upon request

DESCARTES
AND
HUME

by

EZRA TALMOR

Senior Lecturer in Philosophy, Haifa University, Israel
Docteur de l'Université de Paris
Formerly Associate Member of St. Antony's College, Oxford

PERGAMON PRESS

OXFORD · NEW YORK · TORONTO · SYDNEY · PARIS · FRANKFURT

U.K.	Pergamon Press Ltd., Headington Hill Hall, Oxford OX3 0BW, England
U.S.A.	Pergamon Press Inc., Maxwell House, Fairview Park, Elmsford, New York 10523, U.S.A.
CANADA	Pergamon of Canada, Suite 104, 150 Consumers Road, Willowdale, Ontario M2J 1P9, Canada
AUSTRALIA	Pergamon Press (Aust.) Pty. Ltd., P.O. Box 544, Potts Point, N.S.W. 2011, Australia
FRANCE	Pergamon Press SARL, 24 rue des Ecoles, 75240 Paris, Cedex 05, France
FEDERAL REPUBLIC OF GERMANY	Pergamon Press GmbH, 6242 Kronberg-Taunus, Pferdstrasse 1, Federal Republic of Germany

---

First edition 1980

British Library Cataloguing in Publication Data

Talmor, Ezra
Descartes and Hume.
1. Hume, David
2. Descartes, René
I. Title
192   B1498   79-41748
ISBN 0-08-024274-X

In order to make this volume available as economically and as rapidly as possible the authors' typescripts have been reproduced in their original forms. This method has its typographical limitations but it is hoped that they in no way distract the reader.

*Printed and bound in Great Britain by
William Clowes (Beccles) Limited
Beccles and London*

To
My Mother

Analytical Contents

II METHODIC DOUBT AND MITIGATED SCEPTICISM

VI   HUMEAN ETHICS

Preface

The aim of this book is to try to understand how Hume
could make an objective picture of man, society and
nature, from purely subjective elements: ideas. This
question naturally leads to Descartes, the inventor
of the new use of the term 'idea'. Was Descartes a
rhetorician? Obviously not, since he rejected rhetoric
as unteachable and further, as unnecessary for the
discovery of truth.

The book explores how Descartes, with his new use of
the term 'idea', effectuated a conceptual reform
which was successful as a safeguard against what he
called the prejudices acquired during childhood and
fostered by Scholastic philosophy. These received
opinions being attached to words, were perpetuated
through language. But, instead of inventing a new
universal language which would express the principles
of the new physics, Descartes contented himself with
a very simple and economical invention, the Cartesian
'idea' which embodied these principles: the distinction
between body and mind.

The book shows how Hume by inventing the new use of
the term 'cause' could formulate his doctrine of
necessity as a sequel to the Cartesian doctrine of
ideas. The Humean concept of causality saved, eventually, Cartesianism from the difficulties implied
in the notions of substance and of power.

Finally the book ends by showing that Hume's theory
of ethics is a logical development of both the doctrine
of necessity and of the doctrine of ideas. With the
first doctrine Hume could prove that moral standards

are developed by experience and consist in a sense
for the public good, and with the second doctrine he
could show that moral distinctions are a matter of
sentiment and not of reason.

CHAPTER I

Was Hume a Cartesian?

In his outstanding biography of David Hume, Ernest
Mossner gives us the reasons which led the young Hume
to move from Reims to La Flèche during his three year
stay in France. It seems that life in La Flèche was
much cheaper than in Reims. It is true, Mossner adds,
that the Jesuit College of La Flèche where Descartes
had studied was still a centre of Cartesianism and
hence,

> "perhaps the ideal place in which an anti-Cart-
> esian might rusticate." [1]

It is evident that Mossner does not want to challenge
the usual distinction made in the History of Philosophy between a rationalist like Descartes and an extreme empiricist like Hume. However, one must guard
against the confusion between the opposition within
the Cartesian camp after the Cartesian revolution,
and the opposition put up against Cartesianism by
scholastic philosophers. Thus it is safe to advance
the view that modern historians do consider Hume as
an anti-Cartesian but only in the first sense: an
anti-Cartesian who has already accepted some basic
principle which characterises the innovation made by
Descartes in philosophy.

In the *Treatise*,[2] the *Enquiries*,[3] and the *Essays*,[4] Hume
stresses more than once what he calls "that famous
doctrine" or "the discovery" or "the most profound
philosophy" (*Essays* 168, T 469, E 154). Before we
bring in full what Hume calls the doctrine, discovery
or most profound philosophy, we must insist that he
qualifies its import every time he mentions it. The
qualification amounts to a warning to his readers
that the discovery has no bearing whatsoever on action

1

and conduct. Hume's warning is very puzzling since
practically all his philosophy is based on the doctrine, to the extent that one could say that Hume
pursues both in the *Treatise* and the *Enquiries* one
single aim which is the *evolvement out of the doctrine of
all its logical conclusions*. But he does not repeat these
warnings every time he infers yet another startling
discovery from his "dogmatic" doctrine. What is the
doctrine?

> "That tastes and colours, and all other sensible
> qualities, lie not in the bodies, but merely in
> the senses"

and the warning:

> "This doctrine, however, takes off no more from
> the reality of the latter qualities, than from
> that of the former; nor need it give any umbrage
> either to critics or moralists."

By "former" and "latter" he refers to qualities of
bodies on the one hand and to qualities of works of
art and of men on the other. He even goes further
in the *Essays* which are meant for the general reader
and not for the reader accustomed to philosophical
speculations and comforts his readers:

> "Though colours were allowed to lie only in the
> eye, would dyers and painters ever be less regarded
> or esteemed? .... And as it is certain, that the
> discovery above mentioned in natural philosophy,
> makes no alteration on action and conduct, why
> should a like discovery in moral philosophy make
> any alteration?" (*Essays* 168)

In the *Treatise* and in the *Enquiries* the warning is
very laconic:

> "And this discovery in morals, like that other in
> physics, is to be regarded as a considerable adv-
> ancement of the speculative sciences; tho', like
> that too, it has little or no influence on practice"
> (T 469).

and

> "There is another sceptical topic of a like nature,

derived from the most profound philosophy; which
might merit our attention, were it requisite to
dive so deep, in order to discover arguments and
reasonings, which can so little serve to any serious purpose" (E 154).

Could we say that the "doctrine" in some form or another is what we called the "basic principle" introduced by Descartes or propagated by him, and which
makes us describe Hume as a Cartesian and which makes
us also describe him as an anti-Cartesian because he
introduced some fundamental changes in the "doctrine"?
Many historians would acquiesce to such a broad characterisation of Hume without necessarily limiting
Hume's anti-Cartesianism to his revised form of what
has been called the doctrine of ideas. Many would
point out that the difference between Descartes' Metaphysics of *a priori* principles and Hume's experimental
method could not be understood solely as the difference
between their two versions of the doctrine. Readers
of Hume's writings must have already recognised in
what context Hume brings in the "Doctrine". In the
Treatise Book III Section 1 he is arguing against the
theory that moral distinctions are made by demonstrative or matter of fact reasoning and he mentions the
theory of ideas in order to reinforce his view that
when we pronounce any action or character to be vic-
ious or virtuous this means that we have a feeling
or sentiment of praise or blame from the contemplation
of it. And the usual conclusion of modern readers is
that Hume is arguing for what is called nowadays an
emotive theory of ethics. Both those who hold such
a theory and those who reject it have interpreted the
first two sections of Book III of the *Treatise* as the
application of the "new discovery" (as developed by
Berkeley and Hume, of course) to ethics.

But surely Hume could not be understood to mean that
the development in Physics which he wants to emulate
in Moral Philosophy, was the evolution of Natural
Philosophy towards subjectivism. In his Essay "The
Sceptic" he is very far from such a conclusion:

"In the operation of reasoning, the mind does
nothing but run over its objects, as they are

supposed to stand in reality, without adding any
thing to them, or diminishing any thing from them.
If I examine the Ptolemaic and Copernican systems,
I endeavour only, by my enquiries, to know the
real situation of the planets; that is, in other
words, I endeavour to give them, in my conception,
the same relations that they bear towards each
other in the heavens. To this operation of the
mind, therefore, there seems to be always a real,
though often an unknown standard, in the nature
of things; nor is truth or falsehood variable by
the various apprehensions of mankind. Though all
the human race should for ever conclude that the
sun moves, and the earth remains at rest, the sun
stirs not an inch from his place for all these
reasonings; and such conclusions are eternally
false and erroneous." (*Essays* 166)

It is interesting to note that this passage comes
two pages before the note where he mentions "that
famous doctrine". It would be natural for us to
suspect our way of interpreting Hume's enthusiasm
for the doctrine and it would be equally if not more
natural to regret the equation of the Cartesian doctrine with some form of idealism.

A philosopher holding a theory which declares the
existence of objects in space outside us either to
be merely doubtful and undemonstrable or to be false
and impossible cannot, as Hume does, in the above
quoted passage, affirm the objective nature of laws
of nature and emphasise the independence of this
objective nature of the operations of the understanding.

However, recalling Hume's reduction of the idea of
necessary connexion to an habitual inference in the
mind, it would be rather difficult to ignore what is
the accepted interpretation, viz. that the doctrine
is the major argument for Hume's scepticism. If the
starting point from which we want to reach knowledge
of the external world is an idea in the mind then
scepticism could be the only answer to Descartes'
quest to provide an answer to scepticism. The corres-

pondence model, along which all Cartesians will try
to give a satisfactory answer to the problem of the
possibility of knowledge, has been called by some
"the characteristic obsession of European philosophy".
When in the *Enquiries* Section XII Hume undertakes the
task of surveying the various kinds of sceptical attitudes, the last item he mentions is the sceptical
topic, derived from the most profound philosophy and
says that

> "It is universally allowed by modern enquirers,
> that all sensible qualities of objects, such as
> hard, soft, hot, cold, black, &c. are merely sec-
> ondary, and exist not in objects themselves, but
> are perceptions in the mind, without any external
> archetype or model, which they represent." (E 154)

After that he goes on to deny the existence even of
primary qualities of objects such as extension and
solidity. In the context of any study of Hume's scepticism (not to forget that many consider him as one
of the greatest sceptics[5]), the above passage is considered to be the most devastating argument against
any certainty in our knowledge of the external world.
No wonder that Reid has held Descartes to be responsible for the Empiricists' tenet that what we know
and perceive are only ideas in the mind and not objects and that any knowledge of the latter must be
justified in terms of the former.

And yet Hume has rejected scepticism arguing that
nature has determined us to reason, believe and act,
though we are not able by our most profound enquiries
to satisfy ourselves about the foundations of these
operations. Before going into a more detailed examination of what he meant by "nature has determined
us" it would be worthwhile to stress what he wrote
about liberty and necessity in his philosophical books
and about causality in his *Essays*. For instance, in
his Essay "Of the Rise and Progress of the Arts and
Sciences," after stating his general rule concerning
the study of any subject, he goes on to apply it in
his study of the rise and progress of learing. The
general rule amounts to Hume's conception of deter-
minism:

"What depends upon a few persons is, in a great measure, to be ascribed to chance, or secret and unknown causes: what arises from a great number, may often be accounted for by determinate and known causes." (Essays 112)

In the case of secret and unknown causes it is obvious that Hume's attitude is that of silence; and it seems that in the study of the origin of the Arts and Sciences this should be the case. Those who cultivate the Arts are always few in number and rather than assign causes to the rise of a great poet, causes which never existed, or reduce what is merely contingent to stable and universal principles, it would be better, Hume writes, to attribute the poet's genius to secret and unknown causes. Needless to say that not many scientific or rationalist thinkers nowadays would contradict what Hume says as a matter of preamble to his real view. What follows this cautious introduction is one of the most extreme materialist interpretations and deterministic explanations of the causes of literacy, and of philosophical, artistic, and scientific creativity.

"But there is a reason which induces me not to ascribe the matter altogether to chance. Though the persons who cultivate the sciences with such astonishing success as to attract the admiration of posterity, be always few in all nations and all ages, it is impossible but a share of the same spirit and genius must be antecedently diffused throughout the people among whom they arise, in order to produce, form, and cultivate, from their earliest infancy, the taste and judgment of those eminent writers. The mass cannot be altogether insipid from which such refined spirits are extracted. There is a God within us, *says Ovid*, who breathes that divine fire by which we are animated. Poets in all ages have advanced this claim to inspiration. There is not, however, any thing supernatural in the case. Their fire is not kindled from heaven. It only runs along the earth, is caught from one breast to another, and burns brightest where the materials are best prepared and most happily disposed. The question, therefore, concerning the rise and progress of the arts and sciences is not altogether a question concerning the taste, genius, and spirit

of a few, but concerning those of a whole people,
and may therefore be accounted for, in some measure, by general causes and principles." (*Essays*
114- 115)

We needed this rather long quotation in order to stress
the contrast between the scepticism pervading his
theoretical writings and the extreme positivism which
instructs his practical essays. There is in *Madame
Bovary* the unforgettable character Homais the apoth-
ecary who is used by Flaubert to deride the type of
Comtian dogmatic believers that science can explain
everything and should supersede both religion and
philosophy. Viewed from the vantage point of our
climate of opinion Hume seems to anticipate Homais.
Is it one of those many inconsistencies which now and
again have been detected in Hume's philosophy, e.g.
that on the one hand he melodramatically - at the end
of the first Book of the *Treatise* - reveals his utter
confusion as a result of his philosophical speculations, and on the other he dogmatically asserts that
all causes are necessary and that one could find these
necessary causes even in the case of poetical genius?
Taking into account his belief that superstition is bad
and that belief in any supernatural origin of mental or
physical phenomena must be rejected, one is led to
the conclusion that there must be in Hume's thought
some "hidden connexion" between what we take to be
scepticism in its most developed form and what we
cannot but consider as an exaggerated confidence in
our capacity to explain all natural and human phenomena in terms of causes and effects. In other words
there is a need to explore more in depth the function
which scepticism fulfills in Hume's philosophy, and,
more specifically, the function of the Doctrine in
relation to his scepticism since by common consent
the former is at the origin of the latter.

It may be asked for instance why did Hume write that
the doctrine is responsible for all the recent progress
in physics? In both Introductions, to the *Treatise* and
to the *Enquiries*, there is no mention of the doctrine
when he expounds his programme of applying the experimental method to moral subjects. We are given to
understand that his plan is inspired by the astonishing

revolution which has occurred in the domain of Natural
Philosophy and that he wants to copy the method of
experiment and observation which is responsible for
the revolution in Astronomy and Physics. He even
anticipates some of the most recent reservations concerning the possibility of experimentation in human
matters. So one is led to ask the question about
the relation between Hume's notion of experimental
philosophy which we understandably admit as a reas-
onable explanation of the advances in physics, and
the doctrine of ideas which we cannot consider but
as conducive to scepticism in regard to science. How
then could Hume see the Doctrine as responsible for
the development of modern physics?

The relation between experimental philosophy and the
notion of experience in terms of sensations, ideas,
perceptions, impressions dates from Descartes. So
a simple explanation of how in Hume's thought experimental philosophy and the doctrine (which says that
qualities are not in the objects but perceptions in
the mind) are related and could both be said to be
responsible for the great advances in physics is that
experience is conceived primarily in terms of sense
perception. Provided the mental realm is distinguished from the material realm and experience is res-
olved into perceptions, it is understandable that
Hume could attribute the progress of physics to the
experimental method or to its equivalent the doctrine.

In the Introduction to the *Treatise* Hume assumes that
the progress of all the sciences is dependent on our
knowledge of our intellectual capacities and of the
limit of these capacities. We cannot go beyond our
capacities, or, in Hume's words

> "'tis still certain we cannot go beyond experience,"
> (T XXl)

Just as we cannot talk of qualities and powers in
external objects of which we have no ideas we cannot
talk about the essence of the mind. Since according
to Hume the doctrine is nothing but the most concise
summing up of the rejection by Natural Philosophy of
any talk about hidden and unseen powers and qualities,

it was natural for him to equate the experimental
method with its basic assumption: to rely only on
experience and not to go beyond experience means not
to suppose that qualities are in the objects.

The rejection of ultimate principles must not be
esteemed in the science of man to be a defect: on the
contrary, it is only because in the natural philosophy
scientists have relinquished any talk about *powers,
qualities, or ultimate principles* that they could make the
advances they made in physics. Besides, Hume thought
that the experimental method was dependent for its
successes in natural philosophy on the human capacity
to cease looking for unperceived powers and principles.
So Hume conceived that the science of man if developed
from its implicit form already present in our way of
studying natural phenomena, to its explicit form as
he will do it in the *Treatise*, not only Moral Philosophy will benefit but also Natural Philosophy. The
ultimate picture Hume wants to achieve of Man in his
relation to the Universe, to Nature, is a picture of
man explained by the same causal necessity which explains nature.

One of the main reasons why we cannot understand
Hume's equation of the experimental method with the
doctrine of ideas is of course our reluctance to
admit that a science of human nature - psychology -
could be of any help to science, let alone to philosophy of science. Even if we overlook the problem
of the supposed relevance of psychology to science
or to philosophy, there remains the other formidable
objection to Hume's project to found the science of
man on an introspective and utterly subjective basis.

This brings us to another paradoxical aspect of Hume's
doctrine: how could he think to achieve an objective
scientific view of Nature and of Man, starting as he
did from such purely subjective items as impressions
and ideas in the mind? An objective science of morals
and politics was his ultimate aim but we must not
wait for the *Essays* in order to become aware of this.
Thus in Section VIII of the *Enquiries* "Of Liberty and
Necessity" defending his view that human actions are

subject to causal necessity just as natural events,
Hume writes:

> "Nor have philosophers ever entertained a diff-
> erent opinion in this particular. For, not to
> mention that almost every action of their life
> supposes that opinion, there are even few of the
> speculative parts of learning to which it is not
> essential. What would become of *history*, had we
> not a dependence on the veracity of the historian
> according to the experience we have of mankind?
> How could *politics* be a science, if laws and forms
> of government had not a uniform influence upon
> society? Where would be the foundations of *morals*,
> if particular characters had no certain or deter-
> minate power to produce particular sentiments,
> and if these sentiments had no constant operation
> on actions?" (E 89-90)

It might be possible that if we clarify how Hume
could combine utter subjectivism with an "exaggerated"
objectivism we might understand other contradictions
in his thought such as between scepticism and certainty, the reduction of necessary connexion to an
inference in the mind, the universalisation of the
doctrine of necessity to all phenomena (mental, moral
and physical), the subjectivity of the moral sentiment and the objective existence of the idea of justice
and so on. However, one way which is certainly not
going to help us solve these difficulties in understanding Hume's thought, is the discarding of the
doctrine of ideas as some kind of fashion through
which Hume exposed his theory which could have been
put forward independently of the fashion.

Such a view of the doctrine of ideas is sometimes due
to the great affinity between some of Hume's fundamental conclusions and the philosophical principles
held by some modern and contemporary philosophers.
The affinity is so great that some philosophers have
talked about what they call "the return to Hume".
Such a return makes Hume a precursor of contemporary
philosophy. For instance Logical Positivists and
Ethical Emotivists have repeatedly defended their
conclusions by simply invoking the similarity of their

conclusions with those of Hume. The distinction
between demonstrative reasoning and inductive reasoning which is fundamental in the philosophy of some
modern empiricists (not only Logical Positivists) has
been found to be similar to Hume's distinction between relation of ideas and matter of fact and even
a name has been found for the distinction: "Hume's
Fork".

Similarly, the famous "Is-Ought" passage in Book III
of the *Treatise* has been called "Hume's Law"[6] which
forbids us to draw moral conclusions from factual
premisses. To all these modern contemporary philosophers the Doctrine of Ideas through which Hume has
formulated his "Fork" and his "Law" is simply the
Cartesian notion of the human mind which Descartes
has foisted on philosophers. This doctrine of impressions and ideas is seen as but a doctrine of gho-
stly fragments of a metaphysical ghost which has been
exploded by Hume himself. The elements to which Hume
wants to reduce human experience are Cartesian ideas
without the Cartesian Mind: the simple indivisible substance totally distinct from the other substance, matter.
Modern empiricists reject the equation of experience
to sensations in the mind. We must not assume as a
matter of fact that they condemn Hume's project of
the science of man as totally unfounded. Psychology,
provided it does not start with purely subjective
items which could be known solely by introspection,
is said to be a legitimate science. Positivists of
all kinds assume that the modern methods of physio-
logical and behavioural psychology can in principle
help us to understand man's mental activities.

There is perhaps for us more hope to begin to understand what we have called Hume's contradictory views
if we try to construe the doctrine as a theory of
meaning. Even if this approach to Hume's conception
of our mental activities would involve us in great
difficulties, it has at least, over the selective
approach of the Positivists, the advantage of not
oversimplifying the whole issue: all that is valid
and durable in Hume's philosophy is independent of
what is absurd and ephemeral - and the latter is
entirely due to Descartes.

However, before relating the contemporary analytic
approach to the doctrine of Cartesian ideas, we must
be aware that the Wittgensteinian critique of Cartesians is mainly directed against contemporary Cartesians like Russell and the early Wittgenstein himself. We are alluding to the argument against the
possibility of a private language. Whether the early
Cartesians like Descartes and Hume have really held
a Doctrine which entailed a possibility of a private
language is not an easy matter to decide. It might
be the case that Descartes and Hume were not inter-
ested in the same problems of metaphysics and epis-
temology that worry contemporary philosophers. Though
all the early Cartesians did take the view that language draws its meaning from words referring to ideas
and that reasoning and thinking are not conducted
with words but with ideas, it might be very difficult
to reconstruct their theory of language and their
theory of meaning with our modern conceptual apparatus.
Some writers have assumed that the early Cartesians
did not have at all any theory of meaning and if this
is the case it might well be that the notion of philosophy itself as practised by the early Cartesians
is quite different from analytic philosophy.

In spite of all these warnings there is still a great
virtue in the modern critical approach, since it allows
us to consider Hume's philosophy as a whole. We no
longer need deplore part of his philosophy while
applauding the rest. Hume's concept of experience
as consisting of mental items, his scepticism founded
on the gap between these mental items and the outer
world, his conception of language and of mind, his
doubts about induction, his notion of knowledge and
belief as consisting of mental states, in short all
of Hume's science of man is brought under the criticism of analytic philosophy. At last one can admit
the fact that the famous doctrine to which Hume alludes several times is a central point in his philosophy and informs all his speculations about human
nature. The analytic approach to the doctrine of
ideas starts from the basic assumption that non-public
events in the mind cannot explain our linguistic activity which is public and inter-subjective. Since
our perceptions, beliefs, inferences, knowledge are
in the last instance assessed by the expression of

these perceptions, beliefs, inferences, and knowledge
in language and independently of any mental occurrence
which might or might not accompany them, one can conclude that the Doctrine is misconceived.

Though the notion of privacy is implied or seems to
be implied in the Cartesian way of ideas, there is
in the case of Hume at least reason to doubt that he
conceived perceptions as private events. For instance,
in Section VIII "Of Liberty and Necessity", in a foot-
note, he relates the prevalence of the doctrine of
liberty to a false sensation or seeming experience
of liberty or indifference which we have or may have
in many of our actions. Were this false sensation
of liberty to be true it would be impossible for any
observer to understand, let alone to predict, our
behaviour:

> "And it seems certain, that, however we may imagine
> we feel a liberty within ourselves, a spectator
> can commonly infer our actions from our motives
> and character; and even where he cannot, he con-
> cludes in general, that he might, were he perfectly
> acquainted with every circumstance of our situation
> and temper, and the most secret springs of our
> complexion and disposition. Now this is the very
> essence of necessity, according to the foregoing
> doctrine." (E 94)

It is obvious that Hume thinks that we do not need
to assume the existence of these "secret springs" in
order to understand or predict the behaviour of a
man; what he means is that the mere fact that we
might assume such "secret springs" indicates that
we do not subscribe to the doctrine of liberty. Since
motive and character are understood as perceptions
or a set of mental habits, it is obvious from the
above quotation that Hume construes mental traits in
behaviouristic terms and there is no inbuilt gap
which prevents us from knowing other minds.

So we are back again to the same puzzle: that what
we interpret as an inbuilt gap between evidence and
belief or knowledge of the external world, what we
take to be an inherent scepticism in the Doctrine,

what we suppose to be eminently private in Cartesian
ideas, might all be the effect of our way of understanding with our own concepts a philosophy which
was not troubled by "gap", "scepticism", and "privacy"
as our philosophy is. Wittgenstein alludes to the
possibility of a gap between our concept of philosophy
and that of the Cartesians when he reflects on his
own way of philosophising:

"Every particular notation stresses some particular point of view. If e.g. we call our investigations 'philosophy', this title, on the one hand,
seems appropriate, on the other hand it certainly
has misled people. (One might say that the subject we are dealing with is one of the heirs of
the subject which used to be called 'philosophy'.) [7]

And of course one might well ask if the "conjuring
trick" he imputes to the Cartesians when they talk
about mental states and processes and leave their
nature undecided, could not be imputed back to the
Wittgensteinians. The way we see the "gap" between
evidence and beliefs, to take one main consequence
of the doctrine of ideas, is imposed *by us* on the
holders of the doctrine. It might be legitimate to
aim at getting rid of the terminology of ideas; but
it is doubtful if it is legitimate to impose on
Descartes and Hume our conceptions of what philosophy is.

It is by now quite evident that there is a "gap"
between our conception of philosophy and that of the
Cartesians and that this "gap" is the cause of our
tendency to write the history of philosophy backwards. It appears then that when we pointed out the
advantage of the analytic critique of the Doctrine of
ideas we were not justifying the critique but only
stressing its power to put into a conceivable whole
its arguments against the whole of Cartesian philosophy. We have left behind all the previous arguments against Hume, arguments that stressed the irre-
levance of psychology to philosophy, or disregarded
what Hume took as the central principle of all his
philosophy, the doctrine, as mere philosophical
jargon. Nevertheless, it might be contended that

the analytic critique also directs its arguments
against the language of ideas and ends up again by
accusing Descartes of some rhetorical trick in order
to commit the British empiricists in general and
Hume in particular to a kind of ontology of occult
mental entities. There is still a decided advantage
for the analytic approach: the tacit hint that what
Hume took to be the function of philosophy is no
longer accepted. This is to say the least. Hume
did not only think that he was exploring the nature
of the experimental method, but also that the method
of philosophy itself was experimental. For him true
Metaphysics was the science of human nature which
included Logic, Ethics, Criticism, and Psychology.
However, most historians, even when they attempt to
explain away his declared intention to study moral
norms by matter of fact reasoning never take Hume's
intention to reduce philosophy to matter of fact reasoning seriously.

On this point it might be said that Descartes' philosophy has always seemed more orthodox than Hume's.
Cartesian rationalism may be found to be based on
some invalid arguments but still it is not misconceived as Hume's experimentalism is. It is true
that some have tried to reconcile in Hume's philosophy the factual observations and generalisations
with his logical analysis. This attempt has usually
taken the form of rejecting the accusation against
him that he confused the factual, the psychological
with the conceptual, without even being aware that
he was making such a confusion. For instance Noxon
has argued that Hume does not found his philosophical
conclusions on a psychological theory but rather
adduces psychological facts which clarify his logical
analysis of causality or the identity of the self.[8]
Nobody has ever tried to do for Hume's philosophy of
the understanding what some moral philosophers have
done for his ethics. Thus MacIntyre has defended
the view that the Is-Ought passage should be construed in the light of Hume's intention of analysing
moral reasoning as a species of matter of fact reasoning.[9] In sum it seems unthinkable to try to justify
Hume's claim that it is by matter of fact reasoning
that he reaches his conclusions concerning the nature

of causal reasoning. For Hume, every discipline
except mathematics (sometimes not including geometry)
was a matter of fact reasoning and the latter could
explain its rise and progress. In the essay which
we have mentioned earlier, "Of The Rise and Progress
of the Arts and Sciences", he includes philosophy
in the list of arts and sciences:

> "Greece was a cluster of little principalities,
> which soon became republics; and being united
> both by their near neighbourhood, and by the ties
> of the same language and interest, they entered
> into the closest intercourse of commerce and
> learning. There concurred a happy climate, a
> soil not infertile, and a most harmonious and
> comprehensive language; so that every circumstance
> among that people seemed to favour the rise of
> the arts and sciences. Each city produced its
> several artists and philosophers, who refused to
> yield the preference to those of the neighbouring
> republics; their contention and debates sharpened
> the wits of men; a variety of objects was presented
> to the judgment, while each challenged the pre-
> ference to the rest; and the sciences, not being
> dwarfed by the restraint of authority, were en-
> abled to make such considerable shoots as are
> even at this time the objects of our admiration."
> (E 121-122)

However, one might well accept Hume's explanation in
terms of causes and effects of the rise of Greek
philosophy without concurring with his other cont-
ention that philosophical arguments are causal arguments. What really strikes the reader of the *Essays*
much more than of the *Treatise* or the *Enquiries* is how
strange is the interest of Hume in the History of
the creative intellect. We are very far nowadays
from this kind of interest which anyway can well
distract us from our main interest: the study of the
product of the creative mind. It is immaterial for
us to study the history and causes of Descartes'
creativity, supposing it were possible to conduct
such a problematic enquiry: we are too much aware
of the immense obstacles and difficulties we have
to surmount and even when surmounted the result of
our enquiry would not necessarily help us in under-

standing the *Meditations*. But Hume's interest in the
history of the creative mind, and how it depends on
the kind of political regime, artists, scientists,
and philosophers live under, is not totally overlooked when he is studying human understanding or
ethics. When in the Introduction to the *Treatise* he
writes about the importance of the Science of Man he
is fully convinced that if we know how we create in
intellectual matters, that is if we know how we reason, then we can also improve our creativity in all
the fields where intellectual capacity matters:

> "'Tis evident, that all the sciences have a rela-
> tion, greater or less, to human nature; and that
> however wide any of them may seem to run from it,
> they still return back by one passage or another.
> Even *mathematics, natural philosophy, and natural religion,*
> are in some measure dependent on the science of
> Man; since they lie under the cognizance of men,
> and are judged of by their power and faculties.
> 'Tis impossible to tell what changes and improve-
> ments we might make in these sciences were we
> thoroughly acquainted with the extent and force
> of human understanding, and could explain the
> nature of the ideas we employ and the operations
> we perform in our reasonings." (T XIX)

We are indeed very far with our concept of philosophy
and even farther with our concept of the *uses* of
philosophy from Hume's ambitious philosophical aims.
However, this does not preclude us from judging Hume's
philosophy by our own standards of the logical analysis of concepts. Columbus might well have never
known that he had landed in America, he might even
have died convinced that he had landed in India, and
three centuries later a new discoverer might have come
and shown that he was wrong. Creativity might be a
process which could be studied experimentally but an
intellectual creation is to be assessed and judged by
some standard; and if this creation happens to be
about logic how could it be judged but according to
our notion of logic? The trouble is that Hume was
well aware of the importance of standards in criticism,
morals and in logical reasoning as well, and he took
the view that these standards are universal and permanent; but he maintained that the foundations of

these standards can be explained by matter of fact
reasoning. Could we answer him, that even if the
origin of standards of criticism is an experience,
this does not entail that the application of these
standards is a matter of experience rather than of
logical analysis? One could surmise that Hume's answer would be negative: philosophical, moral and
critical arguments are all of experimental origin,
they improve with practice, unlike mathematical reasoning. One could imagine Hume accepting the argument
that a causal history of say philosophy, does not
entail that philosophical arguments are matter of
fact reasoning; but it seems quite impossible that
he would have agreed to the proposition that philosophy is essentially conceptual analysis in spite
of the fact that standards of arguments in philosophy
are matter of fact standards. One could even venture
to say that had Hume been living today, and taking
part in philosophical debates about the status of
ethics, or whether there is or there is not a distinction to be made between logical necessity and physical necessity - he would not have changed his mind.

It would be however wrong to infer from the above
argument that the study of a classical text in philosophy by way of arguments is necessarily distorting.
On the contrary, besides being consonant with our
way of doing philosophy at a second remove from any
practical aim, the conceptual analytic method has
many advantages. Such a method is very successful
in enlivening any historical subject like Hume's
Essays and addresses him as if he were present in a
faculty seminar. It ensures the largest number of
participants provided with a minimum of logical training. Last but not least, it introduces a radical
change in the dreariness of the usual textbooks of
history of philosophy which are mainly a nomenclature
of a philosopher's ontological beliefs. As we re-
marked earlier, it may sometimes be selective in its
choice of items discussed but it never relapses into
a list of "isms".

Having said that, we must not forget that the interest
in arguments only can become an obsession too, which
can end in yet another reduction of the study of a

classical text to a list of arguments. And it does
not matter if the historian makes his list very long
and enriches it with a comparison of say Descartes'
arguments with those of contemporary philosophers.
Such a list of arguments stifles the life of the
philosopher's project, it divorces it from its sus-
taining beliefs. The latter are called "intrinsic
beliefs" and are considered irrelevant in the history
of philosophy. They might be relevant in a book
dealing with the history of ideas and what these ideas
meant for the contemporaries of the philosopher concerned. Nevertheless, a philosopher's belief might
be more intimately connected with his philosophical
arguments than the political, economic and geogra-
phical conditions which Hume thought to be the causes
of the creation of this philosophy. What seems puzzling in recent philosophical analysis is that many
philosophers, while maintaining strongly that philosophy is quite distinct from science, equally maintain (or try at all cost to reach) the standard of
a value-free scientific discipline. It is not our
intention here to advocate the practice of a philosophy "engagee". Our concern is with the understanding of Descartes' and Hume's thought and if we
can show that their so-called "extrinsic beliefs"
are indispensable for our understanding, then at
least in their case we would have shown that these
beliefs were not extrinsic at all, but form an int-
egral part of their philosophy.

An interest in Hume's belief, for instance, in the
evil effects of superstition and the consequent
belief that only philosophy can counteract superstition, can help us articulate in a different light
his interest in the causes of intellectual creativity.
It might well be the case that some of the great philosophers like Descartes and Hume were not only inter-
ested in the nature of the creative intellectual act
but were also in fact themselves creators, innovators.
We do not mean by creators or innovators any philosopher who coins new words, or even new systems. In
the past we had too many of the latter and nowadays
we have too many of the former. We mean by a creator
or innovator a thinker who by his writings effectuates
a fundamental change in the practice and understanding

of an intellectual discipline. We shall deal with
Descartes' innovations, which anyway are universally
acknowledged, in the next chapter. As for Hume's
innovations they consist simply in that after he had
written all his books, the concepts of experience,
of cause, of necessity could no longer be the same
as before he wrote. Far from being the case that
he has diluted the notion of causal necessity, he
was the main agent in transforming the notion of
causal necessity into a doctrine of necessary causes
as against the idea of the contingency of causes on
which superstition throve so well.

In other words, an innovator in philosophy just as
in any other field of knowledge must, in order to be
said to have succeeded, introduce a new standard of
appraisal in the subject of his enquiry. The question
to be asked is obviously whether a new standard could
be introduced by limiting oneself to arguments or
logical analysis. And our question becomes more to
the point when we ask ourselves whether we can understand a classical philosophy which is *admittedly inn-
ovating* by concentrating uniquely on the arguments.
When we extend our analysis of arguments to the point
where we are forced to admit, in the case of Descartes,
that in spite of the doubtful premises from which
he starts and in spite of the invalidity of some of
his central arguments, we are left with the inexplicable greatness of Descartes. We cannot take refuge,
as some do, in a discouraging conclusion, discouraging because very vague and certainly unworthy of
philosophical criticism, that the philosophical work
as a whole and in spite of its logical shortcomings
is great. It is one thing to avoid partisanship at
the level of ideological and political strife, that
is at the level where belief and thinking coalesce
so to say, it is another thing to try to go beyond
logical analysis of arguments and articulate a philosopher's basic beliefs which make him bring about
the kind of conceptual revolution we were attributing
to Hume or to Descartes.

Hume talks also of yet another doctrine, the doctrine
of necessity, and this too needs clarification. And
he must have been well aware of the connotation of

such a word like "doctrine" when he writes of other
doctrines which he considers as unworthy:

> "There is, in Dr Tillotson's writings, an argument
> against the *real presence*, which is as concise, and
> elegant, and strong as any argument can possibly be
> supposed against a doctrine, so little worthy of a
> serious refutation." (E 109)

And when defending his view of the causal explanation
of human actions he overtly contrasts the Doctrine of
liberty with the Doctrine of necessity:

> "It seems almost impossible, therefore, to engage
> either in science or action of any kind without
> acknowledging the doctrine of necessity, and this
> *inference* from motive to voluntary actions, from
> characters to conduct." (E 90)

In his struggle on the philosophical level against
occultist explanations of intellectual power, Hume
must have been well aware of the limitations of the
effective powers of arguments. He must have been
equally aware that in order to persuade others that
we do not live in a world full of witches, demons,
and all sorts of supernatural beings, reason is never
sufficient. No wonder that he did not hesitate to
choose *his own doctrines* the *doctrine of ideas* and the
concomitant *doctrine of necessity* in order to fight
against the return of occultist explanations of mental activities and their concomitant theories of
contingent causes.

In this connection it is instructive to compare Hume's
notion of causality with Joseph Glanvill's views on
the same subject. Glanvill wrote his books in the
second half of the seventeenth century and many historians have noted the similarity of their views: he
has even been called a Precursor of Hume.[10] What was
Glanvill's conception of causes?

> "All Knowledge of Causes is *deductive*: for we know
> none by simple intuition; but through the media-
> tion of its effects. Now we cannot conclude, any
> thing to be the cause of another; but from its
> continual accompanying it: for the *causality* it

self is *insensible*. Thus we gather fire to be the
cause of heat, and the Sun of day-light: because
where ever fire is, we find there's heat; and where
ever the Sun is, Light attends it, and *è contrà*. But
now to argue from a concomitancy to a causality,
is not infallibly conclusive: Yea in this way lies
notorious delusion."[11]

If one limits oneself to the theoretical exposition
of Glanvill's view of causality, it is very difficult
to refuse him the title of precursor of Hume. However, when we read his other book on the existence
of witches, *Saducismus Triumphatus* (1689),[12] we find to
what use he puts his notion of causality and thus
realise that he was *not* a precursor of Hume, but on
the contrary one of those metaphysicians against whom
Hume was writing his *Treatise*. Thus Glanvill argues
from concomitancy to the probability of causes in
the sense that any event may be due either to natural
causes or to non-natural causes. And it is this
specific notion of contingent causes which Hume was
combatting with his doctrine of necessity which makes
him declare that all causes are necessary.

Nothing like a comparison between Hume and Reid can
help us understand the gap between us and the early
Cartesians. Reid, a contemporary of Hume, seems to
have lived two or three generations after him. He
acknowledges the debt he owes to Descartes and his
British followers, he is aware that there has been
a revolution:

"The triumph of the Cartesian system over that of
Aristotle, is one of the most remarkable revolutions in the history of philosophy, and has led
me to dwell longer upon it than the present subject required. The authority of Aristotle was
now no more. That reverence for hard words and
dark notions, by which men's understanding had
been strangled in early years, was turned into
contempt, and every thing suspected which was not
clearly and distinctly understood. This is the
spirit of the Cartesian philosophy, and is a more
important acquisition to mankind than any of its
particular tenets; and for exerting this spirit

so zealously, and spreading it so successfully,
Descartes deserves immortal honour."[13]

But unlike Hume, Reid did not seem to worry at all
about all kinds of attempts by various thinkers to
exploit the weakness of the Cartesian system and
reinstitute some form of opaqueness in and about the
mind. Reid is aware that only the transparent way
of talking about our mental operations can help us
to make any progress in the knowledge of the mind
and of nature. He admits that Malebranche, Locke,
Berkeley, and Hume were taught by Descartes how to
distinguish body from mind and consequently how to
reflect accurately on the operations of our own mind.
In sum, Reid starts from the lasting acquisition or
from what he thinks is the lasting acquisition in
philosophy, and goes on to defend his view which is
that we do not need to posit the absurd doctrine of
ideas (ideas as existing items in the mind, directly
perceived, objects known only by the intermediary of
ideas) in order to preserve both the accurate Cartesian reflection on the operations of our mind and
the concomitant distinction between these operations
and the outer world. And the question is of course
whether he could have conceived his *Essays on the Intellectual Powers of Man* were it not for the victory of the
doctrine of ideas over the doctrine of substantial
forms. But while Hume equating as he was philosophy
with the science of man, was still defending the Cartesian achievements against those who exploited Cartesian failures, Reid concentrates only on the achievements and wants to get rid of what we shall try to
show was the weapon which secured those achievements:
the doctrine of ideas. It is ironical to think that in
spite of all Reid's sustained arguments against the
theory of ideas, in spite of his remarkable development of the philosophy of perception, it is quite
debatable whether he would not be classified as a
Cartesian by our modern philosophers of language since
he believed that:

"Words are empty sounds, when they do not signify
the thoughts of the speaker ..." (p. 471)

The new positive way of treating intellectual matters

which Reid adopts in his *Essays* is the outcome of a
long and protracted argument between Cartesians and
pseudo-Cartesians. If we start from the end result,
Reid's *Essays*, then we could perhaps reconstruct the
scenario solely in terms of the new Cartesian theory
of mind and neglect Descartes' contributions to physics and mathematics. This neglect does not mean
that Cartesianism is uniquely characterised by its
philosophy of Mind - far from it; what this neglect
means is, as we shall try to show, that the revolution in science could not have its repercussions on
activities which were not directly affected by science
without getting rid of the "mystery" concerning the
human mind. The means to get rid of any occult
quality of the human mind was solved by physicists
like Galileo and the young Descartes (before he became the metaphysician we know) simply by studying
natural phenomena without the anthropomorphic or
animistic substantial forms and species of all sorts.
But not every one was a physicist and hence there
was a need, both in order to protect the new paradigm
of the scientists and in order to make the same paradigm not to appear absolutely esoteric in the eyes
of the layman, to "sterilise the human mind" against
any resurgence of animistic and anthropomorphic instincts.

Whether Descartes did it by a "conjurer's trick", or
by a new "dogma of the Ghost in the Machine" or simply
by a new doctrine, the "doctrine of ideas", or by
some rhetorical innovation, we shall examine in the
next chapters. Not all philosophers accepted the
Cartesian picture of mind, for instance More and his
young disciple Glanvill, enthusiastic as they were
about Descartes' physics and mathematics, will never
adopt his views concerning the nature of the mind.
Religious, Platonic, Renaissance magical influences
might have prevented both More and Glanvill (to mention only two) to accept the Cartesian way of talking
about the mind. Their belief in witches, demons,
spirits dictated to them a concept of mind which
could detect or perceive these witches, demons and
spirits. This Hume saw very clearly and very acutely;
and he felt that if the Cartesian picture of the universe and of man is to be preserved then he should

get rid of what is inessential and preserve what is
essential in this picture. We know too well what
was inessential and what was the source of all the
return to strange beliefs and superstition: the
notion of substance and the notion of hidden power.
Who knows, perhaps Hume's stay at La Flèche helped
him and inspired him to save Cartesianism from its
own errors?

NOTES

1. E.C. Mossner, *The Life of David Hume*, Nelson, 1954,
   p.99.

2. David Hume, *A Treatise of Human Nature*, ed. L.A.
   Selby - Bigge, Oxford University Press, Oxford,
   1888; 1968. Referred to as T.

3. David Hume, *Enquiries Concerning the Human Understanding
   and Concerning the Principles of Morals*, ed. L.A. Selby
   - Bigge, Second Edition, Oxford University Press,
   Oxford, 1902; 1970. Referred to as E.

4. David Hume, *ESSAYS Moral Political and Literary*, Oxford
   University Press, Oxford, 1963; 1974. Referred
   to as *Essays*.

5. See, for example, Richard H. Popkin, "David Hume:
   His Pyrrhonism and His Critique of Pyrrhonism,"
   in *HUME: A Collection of Critical Essays*, ed. V.C.
   Chappell, Anchor Books, Doubleday, New York,
   1966, pp. 53-98.

6. See R.M. Hare, "Universalisability," *Proceedings of
   the Aristotelian Society*, LV (1954-55), p. 303.

7. Ludwig Wittgenstein, *The Blue and Brown Books*, Blackwell, Oxford, 1969, p. 28.

8. James Noxon, *Hume's Philosophical Development: A Study
   of his Methods*, Clarendon Press, Oxford, 1973.

9. A.C. MacIntyre, "Hume on 'Is' and 'Ought'", *Hume*,
   ed. V.C. Chappell, pp. 240-264.

10. See Richard H. Popkin, "Joseph Glanvill: A Pre-
    cursor of Hume", *Journal of the History of Ideas*, XIV
    (1953), pp. 292-303.

11. *The Vanity of Dogmatizing: The Three 'Versions'* by Joseph Glanvill, with a critical introduction by Stephen Medcalf, The Harvester Press, Hove, Sussex, 1970, p. 190.

12. Joseph Glanvill, *Saducismus Triumphatus*, London 1689, A Facsimile Reproduction with an Introduction by Coleman O. Parsons, Gainesville, Florida, 1966.

13. Thomas Reid, *Essays on the Intellectual Powers of Man*, Introduction by Baruch A. Brody, M.I.T. Press, 1969, Reproduced from *The Works of Thomas Reid*, 1814, p. 150.

CHAPTER II
Methodic Doubt and Mitigated Scepticism

In a book by Richard A. Watson, called *The Downfall of Cartesianism 1673-1712*, the author concludes as follows:

"In a wider philosophical context, then, Cartesianism inherited the traditional likeness principles and the ontology of substance and modification; its inadequacies are germane to the modern failure of substance philosophy. In the narrower compass of the late seventeenth century, the dependence of Cartesians upon the ontology of substance and modification led to their inability to explain how causal interaction takes place between unlike substances, and how ideas make objects which are unlike them known. This inability deriving from conflicts among basic principles in the Cartesian system was the major philosophical reason for the downfall of Cartesianism."[1]

It appears that Watson, like many before him, takes Cartesianism as defined by what Reid has called the "particular tenets" which characterise Descartes' philosophy or the philosophy of some of his followers. Dualism of substances and their interaction, we are asked to believe, are the main source of contradiction which brought down Cartesianism. However, Ryle, writing in 1949, some two hundred years and more after the date which marks the downfall of Cartesianism according to Watson, complains that Cartesianism is still the official theory of mind:

"There is a doctrine about the nature and place of minds which is so prevalent among theorists and even among laymen that it deserves to be described as the official theory. Most philosophers, psychologists and religious teachers subscribe, with minor reservations, to its main articles and, although they admit certain theoretical difficulties in it, they tend to assume that these can be overcome without serious modifications being

27

made to the architecture of the theory. It will
be argued here that the central principles of the
doctrine are unsound and conflict with the whole
body of what we know about minds when we are not
speculating about them."

And then Ryle goes on to tell us who is responsible
for this state of affairs which has lasted for *three
hundred years:*

"The official doctrine, which hails chiefly from
Descartes, is something like this. With the
doubtful exceptions of idiots and infants in arms
every human being has both a body and a mind.
Some would prefer to say that every human being
is both a body and a mind. His body and his mind
are ordinarily harnessed together, but after the
death of the body his mind may continue to exist
and function". [2]

No wonder if Cartesianism is both dead and alive
that Ryle is brought to coin his famous metaphor for
the still living - after death - doctrine of ideas
as "the dogma of the Ghost in the Machine". Surely
the "Ghost of Descartes" is held responsible for the
"Ghost in the Machine".

There seems to be more of a gap between us and Descartes than there is between Hume and us. Hume was
developing the Doctrine of ideas, correcting and
adding to it his theory of beliefs, and, in formulating his theory of necessary connexion, he mod-
ified Cartesianism in such a manner that some contemporary philosophers could genuinely say - at least
with partial truth - that their philosophy was in
a way a Return to Hume. Could someone say the same
in relation to Descartes? If we are to listen to a
logical positivist or more generally to some philosopher of science then, in case he does see some
similarity between his philosophy and that of Hume,
he will certainly add the qualification that he means
Hume the Empiricist but not the Cartesian. We have
to admit therefore that Descartes belongs to the
History of Philosophy and that nobody would cons-
ciously call himself a Cartesian nowadays. On the

other hand - and this is surely a sign of the greatness of Descartes - we cannot but conclude by our
reading of Wittgenstein and Ryle for example, that
Descartes' way of thinking is living within us - in
a word, we cannot whenever we talk about our mental
capacities but talk in Cartesian terms.

There was no lack of great philosophers in the 17th
century who adhered to the new mechanical philosophy
which was the main carrier of the revolution against
Aristotelian physics. Robert Lenoble, in his interesting book *Mersenne*, stresses this point mentioning
Mersenne, Gassendi and Hobbes as the possible altern-
atives to Descartes in the vital function of expressing through their philosophy the revolutionary ideas
of the New Science of Galileo and of the New Astronomy
of Copernicus and Kepler. Lenoble deplores the fact
that it had to be Descartes whose name posterity will
link with Science and hence with the founding of
Modern Philosophy. Lenoble's explanation is very
laconic: the need for a metaphysical system to replace
Aristotelian metaphysics provided Descartes with the
unique opportunity to put forward his own Metaphysics.[3]
In the 18th century Condillac and Voltaire will declare their preference for Locke against Descartes -
again because the latter was too metaphysical while
the former was seen as offering a straightforward
description of the operations of the mind without
encumbering them with inexplicable substances.

In the first chapter we hinted that some modern historians unlike Condillac and Voltaire query why Locke
and the other empiricists had to resort to the terminology of ideas in order to develop their experimental philosophy. Thus sometimes we are given to
understand by the metaphysics of Descartes his system
of dualistic substances and their interaction, but
sometimes we are told that the doctrine of ideas with
or without substances is enough to make Descartes a
metaphysician. Recalling Hume's concluding paragraph
in the first *Enquiry* and his condemnation of metaphysics, it is easy to understand how rooted the
view of Hume's anti-Cartesianism is. Nevertheless,
not all writers on Descartes underline mainly his
Methaphysics, on the contrary, most of them stress

what they call the Cartesian epistemological revolution or, to be more exact, they stress how Descartes
has revolutionised philosophy by placing at its centre
the epistemological question "How do I know?" According to this way of seeing Descartes, he was the
first to try to abandon the traditional question of
his predecessors about what the world was like by
insisting that we must first ask how can we know
what the world is like. They further explain that
Descartes' answer was that there was only one method
of answering these questions, the method of beginning
from clear and distinct ideas, the only things which
cannot be doubted, and then build our knowledge in
function of these ideas. In contrast to his empiricist disciples, Descartes still clung to some scholastic elements in his building of the foundations
of knowledge: he resorted to the existence and intuitively known nature of God.

Russell too sees that there is in Descartes' philosophy some unresolved inconsistency between his
attempt to build a philosophy in the age of science
and the remnant of his scholasticism which he had
been taught at La Flèche. However, Russell's insistence on the logical component as the principal ingredient in any philosopher's thought, together with
his conviction that the philosophy of logic thrives
on antinomies, paradoxes, and inconsistencies leads
him to welcome in the last resort Descartes' inconsistencies. Had Descartes tried and succeeded to be
a more complete logical philosopher he would have
simply been the founder of a new scholasticism.
Fortunately his inconsistency made him the origin
of two divergent schools of philosophy: the contin-
ental Rationalist school of Spinoza and Leibniz and
the British Empiricist school of Locke, Berkeley and
Hume.

In general no one questions the fact that Descartes
is responsible for a drastic change in the direction
of Western Philosophy, but whereas a minority of
commentators deplore this change and are trying hard
to undo the harm Descartes has done, most of them
think that Descartes' theory of knowledge and his
theory of human nature which goes with it, his con-

cepts of an idea and of mathematical laws of nature
are so rooted in our modern consciousness that it
is difficult not to see them as the natural property
of the human mind when actually they were created
mainly by Descartes.[4]

One of the difficulties encountered by anyone trying
to show the importance of Cartesianism in the philosophy of Locke or Hume is the received interpretation that Descartes in the *Meditations* uses the
method of doubt and ends up with a quasi - total
scepticism regarding the senses: our knowledge is
grounded mainly on innate ideas of which we are
intuitively aware. Cartesian ideas are seen by many
as concepts while Locke's or Hume's ideas are perceptions, images, impressions, in short some occurrence in the mind. The further description of Descartes' system as rationalistic, metaphysical, deductive, and a *priori* has increased the contrast between Descartes' use of the term "idea" and Hume's.
It is our suggestion that perhaps a re-reading of
the first *Meditation* with the re-reading of the appropriate sections from Hume on Scepticism could throw
some light on both the nature of the method of doubt
and on Hume's scepticism. As we have already hinted
in our first chapter, there is a basic difficulty
in accepting the view that Hume was a sceptic, since
even if we take Hume's scepticism as a mitigated
scepticism, in the sense in which we understand
"mitigated", we cannot reconcile it with the dogmatic
positivism we alluded to in his theory or Doctrine
of necessity (all causes are necessary, none are
contingent) and his application of this doctrine in
his essays on historical and aesthetic matters.

The same applies to Descartes. It is a well-known
argument which says that Descartes never succeeded
in vanquishing the malignant scepticism which he
deploys in the first *Meditation*. Descartes may be
a rationalist but the basis of his rationalism appears
to many as very shaky, personal, subjective, and
incommunicable. Our aim is to compare Descartes'
scepticism with Hume's and show the rhetorical function of their arguments.

We have already conceded that the analytic way of
writing the history of philosophy has many advantages but we have also pointed out some of its draw-
backs. Most contemporary analytic studies while
enlivening in a striking manner Descartes' ideas
appear in the long run to be rather a series of
stereotyped arguments - each commentator choosing
not necessarily the same set of arguments. Russell
seems to have started this tradition of looking at
a past philosopher as a suitable exercise for his
own principles - in his case logical arguments in
the main. But nevertheless for Russell, at least,
philosophy is an attempt to understand the world,
while many other interpreters of Descartes seem to
have relinquished this ambitious aim and settle for
a much more restricted aim of philosophy. By and
large the aim of philosophy is never set higher than
an analysis of the language of science - a secondary
activity, and sometimes it is reduced to the arduous
task of clarifying our concepts, dissolving our
puzzles, and in no case derogating from the supreme
principle of never competing with science. In certain cases the distinction of science from philosophy
takes the form of giving the latter the function of
evolving a system of metaphysics - descriptive metaphysics - which is presupposed by common usage.

So on the whole, the main drawback of the analytic
approach to the history of philosophy is that philosophy is seen as the "material" on which students
exercise their logical ability. No study is considered to be good if it does not take into account
the latest item in logical virtuosity which has just
appeared in one of the latest studies or analyses
in the philosophy of logic, mind, or language. Thus
articles on Descartes must raise the question whether
the Cogito is a truth of logic or a "descriptive
statement", or a "performative statement", or an
"incorrigible statement". The latter concepts bring
in their trail the notions of "inference", "self-
contradictory", "presupposition", "is existence a
predicate?". Needless to say that some of the old
arguments already used by the authors of the Objections to Descartes' *Meditations*, are also used by modern
critics like for example "the Cartesian circle",

"the subjectivity of clear and distinct ideas", and
last but not least the queer notion of an existent
idea. While most of the commentators are of the
opinion that Descartes has plagued philosophy with
the problem arising out of the correspondence theory
of truth, others argue that he was assuming a coher-
ence theory of truth. Some begin to challenge the
orthodox view that Descartes was the first to launch
philosophy on the pursuit of indubitable foundations
of knowledge and argue that he was looking for the
foundations of the possibility of knowledge. In
general no problem arises as to the nature of philosophy itself. The so-called a priorism of Descartes
is easily adaptable to an analytic conceptual enter-
prise. No question is asked whether Descartes was
changing the concept of knowledge or working within
our notion of what constitutes knowledge. In no
case can Descartes be said to assimilate philosophy
to a matter of fact inquiry like Hume did. Some
see Descartes as their ancestor in assigning to philosophy a special subject-matter, others take him to
have conceived philosophy and science as continuous.
In both cases his project is conceived and understood
as an analytic conceptual elaboration of the foundations of an absolute notion of knowledge or of the
possibility of knowledge.

But the analytic back-writing of the history of philosophy did not start with the analytic contemporary
philosophers. Étienne Gilson writing about the gen-
esis of the First Meditation argues against what he
calls the definitive significance of the method of
doubt. Conceding that Descartes himself is responsible for this accepted interpretation of the import
of his method and that historians have based their
verdict on the Cartesian text, Gilson nevertheless
maintains that there is yet another aim which is the
object of the First Meditation. Thus Descartes writes
in the synopsis of the *Meditations*:

   "But although the utility of Doubt which is so
   general does not at first appear, it is at the
   same time very great, in as much as it delivers
   us from every kind of prejudice, and sets out for
   us a very simple way by which the mind may detach
   itself from the senses; and finally it makes it

impossible for us ever to doubt those things which
we have once discovered to be true." (HR I 140).[5]

But, adds Gilson, with the exception of the argument
of the *malin génie* all the other arguments in the
First Meditation centre around the validity of the
evidence of the senses:

> "All that up to the present time I have accepted
> as most true and certain I have learned either
> from the senses or through the senses; but it is
> sometimes proved to me that these senses are decep-
> tive, and it is wiser not to trust entirely to any
> thing by which we have once been deceived."
> (HR I 145).

All reference to the illusions of the senses, of
dream and of madness is nothing but a confirmation
of the Cartesian thesis that if the foundations of
knowledge built on sense-evidence are ruined all
knowledge will crumble down.

It is perhaps crucial at this juncture to explain
precisely what Descartes means by "I have learned
either from the senses or through the senses". We
shall accept Gilson's explanation. Preceding the
writing of his *Meditations* Descartes had meditated on
metaphysical problems and elaborated his physics.
At this stage he was convinced yet not persuaded.
His lack of persuasion was due to the survival of
illusions of sensible origin - illusions of which
every man is victim during his youth. Descartes had
slowly persuaded himself of the real distinction of
the soul from the body, by dissolving one after the
other all the real qualities and substantial forms
in the process of constituting a purely mechanistic
physics. This being the case, Gilson comments, it
would have been preferable, in order to persuade and
convince the readers who are complacent in their false
opinions, to start with the exposition of Cartesian
physics. But Galileo's condemnation drove Descartes
to reverse the order of his publications and to offer
the public his metaphysics before his physics. But
if the physics alone can persuade concerning the
metaphysics (which in turn serve as the foundations

for physics) how can the latter coming before the former be accepted?

"C'est pour résoudre ce problème que Descartes a donné au doute méthodique la place et la forme qu'il reçoit dans les *Méditations*, et l'on peut y voir un succédané d'une physique défaillante qui eut demontré mieux que quoi que ce soit la vanité des connaissances sensibles."[6]

Gilson does not deny that Descartes is also looking, by using the method of doubt, for certainty. What Gilson is questioning is the Kantianisation of Descartes who is seen as "ein Erkenntnistheoretiker wie Kant".

It is now the time to interrupt for a while Gilson's account of the function of Methodical Doubt and start our proposed comparison of the method with Hume's scepticism. We shall concentrate mainly on Section XII of the *Enquiries* which has the advantage of being a compact presentation of Hume's reflections on sceptical topics. We have already mentioned in the first chapter how Hume speaks of the doctrine of ideas in the *Treatise* and stresses its importance for physics. It is worthwhile re-quoting it in full:

"Vice and virtue, therefore, may be compared to sounds, colours, heat and cold, which according to modern philosophy, are not qualities in objects, but perceptions in the mind: And this discovery in morals, like that other in physics, is to be regarded as a considerable advancement of the speculative sciences; tho', like that too, it has little or no influence on practice." (T 469)

It must now be clear that what Gilson calls the dissolving of all real qualities and substantial forms which Descartes effectuates in the process of constituting his physics is what Hume calls

"this discovery ... like that other in physics, is to be regarded as a considerable advancement of the speculative sciences."

What is a discovery for Descartes is a doctrine for

Hume, a doctrine which has proved itself: hence he
has no qualms whatsoever to start like Locke and
Berkeley before him, both his *Treatise* and his *Enquiry*,
with the elements whose existence are assumed by the
Doctrine: perceptions of the mind.

And now to Section XII of the *Enquiries* "Of the academical or sceptical Philosophy". Bearing in mind
Gilson's equation of the method of doubt with the
disappearance of all real qualities and substantial
forms in the bodies, e.g. the transformation of these
qualities and forms into illusions of the senses,
and on the other hand Hume's conception of the doctrine of ideas (qualities are not in bodies but are
perceptions in the mind), we shall not be surprised
at all that the Doctrine is also equated in the
Enquiries with the most radical form of scepticism
which surpasses any previous scepticism. No wonder
that most commentators have considered the famous
passage where Hume writes about a sceptical topic
derived from the most profound philosophy (in other
words the doctrine) as the most devastating sceptical
argument ever used and for which Hume has been called
one of the greatest sceptics in the history of philosophy.

Nothing in this section of the *Enquiry* indicates that
Hume wants to use this absolute doubt which is equivalent to all intents and purposes to the doubt generated by the hypothesis of the *malin génie* in the
First Meditation. There is a complete separation in
the method of presentation of both the *Treatise* and
the *Enquiry* between a) the Doctrine of Ideas as the
famous discovery in physics and which Hume wants to
apply to moral philosophy, and b) the same doctrine
as the source of radical doubt. Besides as we have
noted earlier, Hume's philosophy gives the appearance of being a straightforward debunking of the function of reason in favour of the data of the senses,
of feeling, while the method of doubt is equated with
the vindication of reason against the illusions of
the senses. So in the end one is left with the conclusion that the latest advances in Physics are based
on the most extravagent scepticism ever conceived!

The argument of the Section on "Of the academical or
sceptical Philosophy" advances by stages through
which Hume wants to review the different kinds of
sceptics. Commenting on what he calls *antecedent*
species of scepticism "inculcated by Descartes" Hume
argues that if we take seriously Descartes' recommendations of doubting our own faculties we would
never be cured of our doubts. We cannot restore our
reliance on our faculties once we have doubted them
all, because either there is no original principle
which is self-evident and convincing or, if we suppose there is such a principle, it could not be used
by our faculties already disqualified by the doubt.
He ends his argument against Descartes' Method of
Doubt by recommending a mild form of antecedent scepticism which is nothing but what we would call scientific scepticism based on clearly ascertained facts
and the corroboration of any theoretical conclusion
by these facts or by further experiments. As such,
Hume's version of diluted antecedent scepticism is
clearly part of what we call nowadays the scientific
experimental method.

We shall leave aside what Hume calls *consequent* scepticism, consequent to science and enquiry, because
as it will appear later this kind of scepticism is
part of what Hume's philosophical works are intended
to eradicate. Consequent scepticism is the fertile
ground on which modern superstitions thrive and Hume's
philosophy is a sustained argument against the logical foundations of superstitions.

Antecedent and consequent scepticism aside, the first
kind of scepticism Hume deals with is that which has
its origin in the "trite topics" recurring in the
arguments of the sceptics in all ages against the
evidence of the senses. This kind of scepticism is
not a consequent one: it is simply similar to that
related by Descartes at the beginning of the First
Meditation. Both authors do not pretend to innovate,
they are simply relating the different kinds of sceptical attitudes known before their time. However,
these "trite topics" for Descartes and Hume are not
the source of real concern. Descartes writes:

"But it may be that although the senses sometimes
deceive us concerning things which are hardly per-
ceptible, or very far away, there are yet many
others to be met with as to which we cannot reas-
onably have any doubt, although we recognize them
by their means." (HR I 145)

The same with Hume: he thinks that these doubts admit
of easy solutions:

"These sceptical topics, indeed, are only sufficient to prove, that the senses alone are not implicitly to be depended on; but that we must correct their evidence by reason, and by consider-
ations derived from the nature of the medium, the
distance of the object, and the disposition of
the organ, in order to render them, within their
sphere, the proper criteria of truth and falsehood." (E 151)

Hume then proceeds to present what he calls the kind
of scepticism which is caused when men, relying on
the evidence of the senses, always take the very
images presented by the senses to be the external
objects. But the slightest philosophy teaches us
that what is present is only an image in our mind.
Hume describes the faith of men in the existence of
the external world in two different ways: a) when
no language involving images and sensations is available ("the animal creation are governed by a like
opinion"). In this stage

"we always suppose an external universe, which
depends not on our perception, but would exist,
though we and every sensible creature were absent
or annihilated."

b) the second manner of describing our faith in the
existence of the external world - and this stage too
is before the "slightest philosophy" - is in terms
of the technical vocabulary of the *Treatise* and the
Enquiry:

"It seems also evident, that, when men follow
this blind and powerful instinct of nature, they
always suppose the very images, presented by the

senses, to be the external objects, and never
entertain any suspicion, that the one are nothing
but the representations of the other" (E 151).

In one sentence Hume summarises what constitutes the
substance of Section II Part IV Book I of the *Treatise*,
"Of scepticism with regard to the senses." In this
section Hume explains how, although nothing is ever
present to the senses except our perceptions, we con-
trive by our imagination to take these perceptions
to be the external objects. The "slightest philosophy" of the *Enquiry* is of course the whole of Section
III Part IV Book I of the *Treatise:* "Of the antient
philosophy." Ancient philosophy is, to be more exact,
the successive attempts by pre-Cartesian philosophy
to grapple with the problems arising within the
vulgar system of belief which takes the existence of
the external world as a matter of fact (or as Hume
puts it when men take their perceptions to be the
unchanging external object). Faced with the typical
problems of

"The table, which we see seems to diminish, as we
remove farther from it: but the real table, which
exists independent of us, suffers no alteration"

we conclude, armed with "the slightest philosophy"
that

"It was, therefore, nothing but its image, which
was present to the mind." (E 152)

We must note the fundamental difference Hume makes
between the "trite topics" of the old sceptics which
concern the reliability of the senses and the second
topic, when we become aware of the data presented to
the senses as different from the origin of the data.
All the pre-Cartesian philosophy is nothing according
to Hume but the unsuccessful attempt to protect the
natural belief in the existence of objects by positing
both the object and its image in the mind. Ancient
philosophy far from resolving our doubts concerning
our senses has been the greatest source of scepticism,
and this is mainly due to the fact that it creates
problems which human power cannot solve. It is not
humanly possible to determine how images are caused

by external objects, entirely different from them,
though resembling them. Perhaps they are caused by
the energy of the mind itself:

"It is achnowledged, that, in fact, many of these
perceptions arise not from anything external, as
in dreams, madness, and other diseases." (E 153)

Proceeding with Gilson's hint that the method of
doubt is a surrogate for teaching the readers
Descartes' new physics (which has completed the
divorce of science from real qualities and substantial forms), we could easily see the second step of
the method of doubt (the argument that he might be
dreaming while awake and thus it is possible that
what he believes is as unreal as in dreams) as equivalent to what Hume calls the scepticism resulting
from the attempt of ancient philosophy to cure scepticism. The dream-doubt serves Descartes as a bril-
liant metaphor of the so-called sophistication of
ancient philosophy in comparison to children's instinctive belief in the existence of objects. Nothing
like dreams can give the reader of the *Meditations* a
hint of what is an entirely imaginary thought. Moreover, our equation of the dream-doubt, the second
stage of the method of doubt in the *Meditations,* with
the second stage of scepticism as historically related
by Hume in the *Enquiry,* is further corroborated by
the way Hume opens his section "Of the antient philosoph
in the *Treatise.* This passage is so important for the
understanding of both Descartes' and Hume's uses of
previous sceptical arguments that it is worth while
to quote it in full:

"Several moralists have recommended it as an
excellent method of becoming acquainted with our
own hearts, and knowing our progress in virtue,
to recollect our dreams in a morning, and examine
them with the same rigour, that we would our most
serious and most deliberate actions. Our character
is the same throughout, say they, and appears best
when artifice, fear, and policy have no place, and
men can neither by hypocrites with themselves nor
others. The generosity, or baseness of our temper,
our meekness or cruelty, our courage or pusill-
animity, influence the fictions of the imagination

with the most unbounded liberty, and discover
themselves in the most glaring colours. In like
manner, I am persuaded, there might be several
useful discoveries made from a criticism of the
fictions of the antient philosophy, concerning
*substances, and substantial forms, and accidents, and occult
qualities;* which, however unreasonable and capri-
cious, have a very intimate connexion with the
principles of human nature." (T 219)

Accordingly, Hume continues in the same chapter to
explore the psychological reasons behind all the
"dreams" of scholastic philosophy, dreams which he
compares to spectres in the dark since it "seeks with
eagerness what for ever flies us; and seeks for it
in a place, where 'tis impossible it can exist."
To conclude, all these illusions are due, according
to Hume, to a trivial propensity of the imagination:

"There is a very remarkable inclination in human
nature, to bestow on external objects the same
emotions, which it observes in itself; and so to
find every where those ideas, which are most present to it. This inclination, 'tis true, is suppressed by a little reflection, and only takes
place in children, poets, and the antient philosophers. ... We must pardon children, because of
their age; poets, because they profess to follow
implicitly the suggesions of their fancy: But
what excuse shall we find to justify our philosophers in so signal a weakness?" (T 224-225)

So, in spite of his psychological explanation of the
ancient philosophers' weakness, Hume cannot excuse
them. The same condemning tone can be detected in
Descartes' letter to l'Abbé de Launay of the 22nd
of July 1641. Alluding to the difficulties which
many experience in trying to distinguish mind from
body, Descartes writes:

"c'est à savoir, que les premiers jugements que
nous avons faits dès notre enfance, et depuis
aussi la philosophie vulgaire, nous ont accoutumés
à attribuer aux corps plusieurs choses qui n'appartiennent qu' à l'âme, et d'attribuer à l'amê
plusieurs choses qui n'appartiennent qu'au

corps; et qu'ils mêlent ordinairement ces deux
idées du corps et de l'âme, en la composition des
idées qu'ils forment des qualités réelles et des
formes substantielles, que je crois devoir être
entièrement rejetée." (Alquié II 353-354)

It is by now clear that most commentators have gone
astray when writing about the second species of philosophical scepticism which Hume mentions after the
"trite topics, employed by the sceptics in all ages."
From par. 116 till par. 121 inclusive Hume is dealing
with ancient philosophy and is not, as many have
inferred, alluding to Descartes, Berkelely or Malebranche. The latter are in question later (par. 122)
when he says that

"There is another sceptical topic of a like nature."

He links these deep and profound philosophical speculations with modern enquirers e.g. natural philosophers, and concludes that the belief in the external
existence of objects is contrary to reason

"If it be a principle of reason that all sensible
qualities are in the mind, not in the object."
(E 155)

When the sceptic is aware that the cause of our perceptions is only a certain unknown, inexplicable
Something, that is when the object of knowledge or the
knowledge of external objects is absolutely doubted
by reason, the sceptic has no longer any job to
fulfil.

This is exactly the situation in which Descartes
finds himself after advancing the hypothesis of the
malin génie. In the First Meditation he writes:

"I shall consider that the heavens, the earth,
colours, figures, sound, and all other external
things are nought but the illusions and dreams
of which this genius has availed himself in order
to lay traps for my credulity." (HR I 148)

With this hyperbolic doubt the itinerary of the
method followed by Descartes reaches its final

station just as historically the last stage of scepticism is, according to Hume, reached with the famous doctrine. Similarly, just as for Hume the doctrine is responsible for the considerable progress in physics, for Descartes the hypothesis of the *malin génie* is responsible for the ousting of the last remnants of "real qualities and substantial forms" which Descartes did away with long before writing the *Meditations*, i.e., when he was writing *Le Monde*.

We shall then allow ourselves to correct Gilson in a matter of detail but which is still of some importance. The method of doubt is not equivalent only to what it is substituted for, in the *Meditations:* the new physics. The method of doubt includes in it a supremely compressed history of scepticism, the scepticism arising out of the attempts of scholastic philosophy to deal with the scepticism of the ancients and then the radical hyperbolic doubt presupposed by modern physics. The reading of Hume's section on scepticism in the *Enquiry* helps us to understand the nature of the hyperbolic doubt introduced by the hypothesis of the *malin génie*, especially if we compare another aspect of Descartes' and Hume's thought which accompanies their presentation of the radical doubt and the doctrine of ideas respectively. Descartes and Hume have always warned their readers that the absolute doubt generated by the practice of modern physics - and which consisted in the apparently innocent statement: "Les noms des qualités sont relatifs à nos sens" and "qualities are not in the objects but perceptions in the mind" - is not meant for the world of practice and action but for the realm of speculation, theory, and more specifically for the reflection on our intellectual powers in relation to the new picture of nature offered by the new science. Thus Descartes brings in the warning just before his suggestion that there might be an evil genius whose whole energies are employed to deceive him:

> "For I am assured that there can be neither peril nor error in this course, and that I cannot at present yield too much to distrust, since I am not considering the question of action, but only of knowledge." (HR I 148)

and Hume in the *Enquiries* adds the remark before mentioning the last topic of scepticism (the doctrine
of ideas)

> "Which might merit our attention, were it requisite
> to dive so deep, in order to discover arguments
> and reasonings, which can so little serve to any
> serious purpose." (E 154)

Both of them are much more explicit later, Descartes
in the *Principles of Philosophy* and Hume in the *Essays.*
Thus Descartes after stating Principle II "That we
ought to consider as false all these things of which
we may doubt" goes on to Principle III "That we ought
not to make use of this doubt for the conduct of life
meantime" and then explains why:

> "But in the meantime it is to be observed that we
> are to make use of this doubt only when we are
> engaged in contemplating the truth. For, as re-
> gards the conduct of our life, we are frequently
> obliged to follow opinions which are merely prob-
> able, because the opportunities for action would
> in most cases pass away before we could deliver
> ourselves from our doubts. And when, as frequently
> happens with two courses of action, we do not per-
> ceive the probability of the one more than the
> other, we must yet select one of them." (HR I 219-
> 220)

In the *Essays,* after stressing the importance of the
doctrine for natural philosophy, Hume goes out of
his way in order to calm the reader that it does not
affect nor make any alteration in action and conduct.
However, the whole of Hume's conclusion of Book I
Of the Understanding in the *Treatise* amounts to his admit-
tance that his application of the Doctrine to moral
reasoning and to the problem of personal identity
did have an inhibitory effect although he had warned
us that it should not. He eventually cures himself
by a dose of action and social intercourse and thus
puts an end to his forelorn state which he describes
as follows:

> "I am first affrighted with that forelorn soli-
> tude, in which I am plac'd in my philosophy, and

fancy myself some strange uncouth monster, who
not being able to mingle and unite in society,
has been expell'd all human commerce, and left
utterly abandon'd and disconsolate." (T 264)

Descartes, at the beginning of the Second Meditation
describes metaphorically the state in which the hyperbolic doubt has left him:

"and, just as if I had all of a sudden fallen into
very deep water, I am so disconcerted that I can
neither make certain of setting my feet on the
bottom, nor can I swim and so support myself on
the surface. I shall nevertheless make an effort
and follow anew the same path as that on which
I yesterday entered ..." (HR I 149)

Hume also, at the beginning of the concluding section
of Book I of the *Treatise*, writes like Descartes that,
in spite of the state he finds himself in after the
first part of his voyage, must bring his voyage to
a happy conclusion:

"But before I launch out into those immense depths
of philosophy, which lie before me, I find myself
inclin'd to stop a moment in my present station,
and to ponder that voyage, which I have undertaken,
and which undoubtedly requires the utmost art and
industry to be brought to a happy conclusion."

And then he goes on to describe practically with the
same kind of Cartesian metaphor his state of mind
after developing what he calls somewhere else "The
sceptical solution of his doubts":

"Methinks I am like a man, who having struck on
many shoals, and having narrowly escap'd ship-
wreck in passing a small frith, has yet the tem-
erity to put out to sea in the same leaky weather-
beaten vessel, and even carries his ambition so
far as to think of encompassing the globe under
these disadvantageous circumstances." (T 263-264)

These metaphors in Descartes' *Meditations* and Hume's
Treatise describing their disarray are not simply a

matter of decoration. Both philosophers felt that
their ideas could be the source of a great danger if
the speculative nature of their radical scepticism
were not stressed and action distinguished explicitly
from philosophical speculation. In the *Discourse*, his
first major book, written in French for non-profess-
ionals, Descartes makes a very discrete allusion to
the Method of Doubt without insisting either on the
motivation for the methodic doubt or the importance
of training oneself in it. According to Gilson, he
thought perhaps to enlarge his account of the method
in the Latin translation of the *Discourse*, but, adds
Gilson

> "la publication des *Méditations* ayant rendu cet
> artifice inutile, la métaphysique du *Discours* est
> demeurée sans sa préface nécessaire et, par con-
> séquent, hors d'état de se faire accepter."

And since as we have already mentioned it, Gilson
sees the method of doubt as an alternative to Cartesian physics and hence as indispensable for the
whole of Descartes' argument, he adds

> "La preuve même de l'existence de Dieu, si forte
> soit-elle dans sa teneur métaphysique, devient
> incapable de convaincre dans un exposé où ni la
> physique, ni le doute méthodique ne sont là pour
> dissiper la confusion fondamentale de l'âme et du
> corps." (*Etudes*   p. 187)

It becomes clear that the methodic doubt as well as
the doctrine of ideas are not, on the speculative
level, simply yet another kind of sceptical topics,
they are not continuous with the scepticism of the
ancients or the built-in scepticism of ancient or
vulgar philosophy. Yet on the practical level both
the methodic doubt and the Doctrine because they are
dogmatic in their formulation can be dangerous since
they are what we call unreasonable in action. The
dogmatism of Descartes has been mentioned by Gassendi
in his objections where he criticises Descartes for
going so far as to assimilate the doubtful to the
false and resort to the hypotheses of the dream-
doubt and of the *malin génie*, hypotheses which Gassendi
thinks nobody is going to take seriously. As for

Hume's dogmatism it is enough to point out that he
calls his formulation of the radical scepticism implied by the new physics "that famous doctrine" and,
as we have already commented in the first chapter,
Hume must have been well aware of the dogmatic connotation of the word "doctrine". So it was the case
of one "dogmatism" against another, of one "doctrine"
against another. This is well summed up by Gouhier,
in the case of Descartes as follows:

> "Par la suite, le'doute méthodique' n'est pas un
> doute sceptique, ceci nullement parce qu'il serait
> un doute non sceptique, mais simplement parce
> qu'il n'est pas un doute."[8]

We are now perhaps more ready than before to unveil the
obscurity concerning the variety of scepticism which
Hume calls "consequent scepticism". Hume, we must
not forget, is always working within the doctrine of
ideas and that explains why he mentions it *en passant*
only and at critical moments in the development of
his philosophy. When for instance he is embarking
on the unfolding of his theory of matter of fact
foundations of the Idea of Justice in Book III
Of Morals, he reminds us of the theory of ideas in
order to distinguish his theory of moral distinctions
as a matter of feeling from other Moral Sense theories
of. For the time being let us assume that Hume holds
dogmatically to the doctrine and that he feels certain
that he has developed the Cartesian way of ideas so
as not to be the source of more doubts but of ending
doubts concerning Man and Reality. But he is also
aware that his confidence in clear and distinct conceptions of Mind, reality and the causal relation
is ultimately based on his acceptance of the two
doctrines of ideas and of necessity. This means of
course that he cannot defend completely by the help
of reason why he accepts these two doctrines. So in
the end Hume is aware that any conclusion concerning
the limitation of the understanding is going to be
used by the sceptic, and for his own aims. Thus near
the end of Section VIII "Of the Idea of necessary
Connexion" in the *Enquiry* Hume is aware that his conception of the nature of the idea of necessary connexion is going to be attacked by the sceptics:

"When we say, therefore, that one object is connected with another, we mean only that they have
acquired a connexion in our thought, and give rise
to this inference, by which they become proofs of
each other's existence: A conclusion which is
somewhat extraordinary, but which seems founded
on sufficient evidence. Nor will its evidence be
weakened by any general diffidence of the understanding, or sceptical suspicion concerning every
conclusion which is new and extraordinary. No
conclusions can be more agreeable to scepticism
than such as make discoveries concerning the weakness and narrow limits of human reason and capacity." (E 76)

Consequent scepticism according to Hume can arise
out of any attempted philosophical solution of the
problems which lead people to scepticism. Ancient
philosophy as such did not want to foster scepticism,
on the contrary, it wanted to cure people of their
doubts; but it simply ended in utter scepticism.
Even Cartesianism has generated scepticism because
it retained some scholastic concepts like substance
and power which were obscure. Consequent sceptics
are therefore parasitic on science and enquiry:

"There is another species of scepticism, *consequent*
to science and enquiry, when men are supposed to
have discovered either the absolute fallaciousness
of their mental faculties, or their unfitness to
reach any fixed determination in all those curious
subjects of speculation, about which they are
commonly employed. Even our very senses are
brought into dispute, by a certain species of
philosophers; and the maxims of common life are
subjected to the same doubt as the most profound
principles or conclusions of metaphysics and
theology. As these paradoxical tenets (if they
may be called tenets) are to be met with in some
philosophers, and the refutation of them in several, they naturally excite our curiosity, and
make us enquire into the arguments, on which
they may be founded." (E 150-151)

Thus on our interpretation of what Hume takes to be

consequent scepticism, all philosophical solutions
of scepticism are consequent scepticisms or could
generate scepticism. Needless to say that what he
calls the sceptical solution of scepticism or as it
has been called by some French commentators "The
Shock Treatment", the Cartesian method of doubt, or
ultimately the doctrine of ideas as Hume as developed and practiced it will be able to sustain and
repulse any onslaught *of its consequent scepticism:*
because, as he says,

> "Nor will its evidence be weakened by any general
> diffidence of the understanding, or sceptical sus-
> picion concerning every conclusion which is new
> and extraordinary." (E 76)

In his *Essays On the Intellectual Powers of Man* (1785)
Thomas Reid tried to show how Hume, using principles
borrowed from Locke and Berkelely, has developed a
system of absolute scpeticism, which leaves no ground
whatsoever to believe any one proposition rather than
its contrary. For Reid, Descartes had done away with
any knowledge based on sense analogy, on what Hume
calls the "inclination to bestow the same emotions,
which human nature observes in itself, on external
objects" and he construes Hume's total scepticism not
as an antidote to the doubtful knowledge of real qualities and substantial forms but simply as an absolute
scepticism. Incidentally, the same happened with Descartes' method of doubt. Conceived in order to replace
the new physics which is constructed by Descartes after
discarding one after another all "real qualities and
substantial forms", both the method and the Cogito generated by it engulf man, according to Descartes' critics,
in a greater scepticism and an egocentric solipsism.

However, both Descartes and Hume remained undisturbed
by these critics. It must have been the case that
for both of them the absolute scepticism involved
either in the methodic doubt or the doctrine of ideas
was seen as such only in relation to the old conception of knowledge. Indeed, they must have felt that
the new physics was a total negation of the old Aristotelian physics, in other words, the new physics

was in so far as our childhood habits are concerned
totally unfamiliar and to accept it we had to consider the familiar as an illusion, as false. Hume
must have been the last great philosopher to live
this conflict between the familiar world of objects
and the unfamiliar world of modern science. In order
to understand the passages where he describes the
conflict between the implications of the new science
and the assumptions of the old, we must remember that
Hume is not a scientist, that he is working towards
the application of the doctrine which is responsible
for the progress in physics to human understanding,
ethics, and criticism, in short to what he calls
Moral Philosophy. At the level of the understanding,
physical laws, laws of nature, are the expression
of necessary connexions, and his doctrine of necessity
(which says that all causes are necessary, that there
are no contingent causes, no hidden powers, or hidden
causal connexions) represents physics.

> "Thus there is a direct and total opposition be-
> twixt our reason and our senses; or more properly
> speaking, betwixt those conclusions we form from
> cause and effect, and those that persuade us of
> the continu'd and independent existence of body.
> When we reason from cause and effect, we conclude,
> that neither colour, sound, taste, nor smell have
> a continu'd and independent existence. When we
> exclude these sensible qualities there remains
> nothing in the universe, which has such an exis-
> tence." (T 231)

In the above passage we can detect the conflict between the *reasonableness* of the senses and the rationality of reason, between the assumptions needed for
practice and action and the implications of speculative thought, and lastly the total opposition of
the old science to the new physics. But unlike
Descartes who was writing the *Meditations* in order to
teach his readers how to discover for themselves the
foundations of the new physics, of the new philosophy,
Hume is writing a speculative treatise about practical philosophy. So he might warn the reader that
his total scepticism towards the old science or more
exactly towards the assumptions of the old science,
does not apply to practice and action but when he

reaches the problems of morals and passions, warnings
are no longer enough: he therefore brings to the
surface the conflict between our assumptions for
action and our assumptions for thinking. In short,
Hume could not - as Descartes had done - put the
problems of morality and of action in brackets, e.g.
adopt a provisional code of morals when he was engaged in founding morality on a new revolutionary
Doctrine.

We are now in a position to understand what Hume
means by "mitigated scepticism". When he begins
reflecting on the intention of what we may call "professional sceptics" he has just mentioned "a sceptical topic, derived from the most profound philosophy". As we have tried to explain it before,
modern philosophy has put an end to all the sceptical consequences of ancient philosophy by presenting the new physics as absolutely negating the
assumptions of the old. The new philosophy is radically sceptical about the ancient. Reason tells
us that all the false science was based on the illusion that impressions are objects. Hume has already
said, in connexion with his discovery concerning the
nature of the idea of necessary connexion, that some
professional sceptics will surely exploit his discovery to disparage reason. So when he brings up
again the Doctrine of Ideas in the form of "another
sceptical topic" he means that the sceptic will use
the Doctrine as a "topic" for his scepticism. Accordingly, we have to understand that for Hume Pyrrhonism is a certain species of philosophy which
wants to mix the conclusions of philosophical speculation with action and practice. His mitigated
scepticism is his answer to the modern Pyrrho who
is bound to arise. If the sceptic directs his attack
on reason by pointing out some of the paradoxical
conclusions of geometry or the science of quantity,
then he is grounding his arguments on absurdities
and contradictions that could easily be avoided by
reducing all mathematical reasoning to relation of
ideas in which nothing but clarity and distinction
prevail. If the New Pyrrho wants to stress the relativism pervading our opinions and their resulting
contradictions and hence the doubtful existence of

objects and facts, he will not succeed because in
action and practice we take facts and objects for
granted and cannot possibly subsist without reasoning
about them. There remains only one domain where the
new Pyrrho might exercise his power and this is Hume's
conclusion concerning causality. There, provided he
remains confined to the philosophical level, the
sceptic can show his force or "his own and our weakness", But if he will insist and try to transfer
his doubts to the realm of action and practice

> "all discourse, all action would immediately cease;
> and men remain in total lethargy, till the nec-
> essities of nature, unsatisfied, put an end to
> their miserable existence." (E 160)

The radical methodic doubt of Descartes which is
excluded from the realm of action and solely applied
in the search of Truth, has resulted in the certainty
of the existence of our thoughts. Hume generalises
the Cartesian methodic doubt and includes in it not
only the search for truth but also the Pyrrhonic
doubt about action, and this will give him the conviction about the narrow capacity of human understanding. Like Descartes' hyperbolic doubt Hume's
Pyrrhonian doubt can be exercised once only and conviction will ensue. In the first case, the existence
of thought is the result of the method of doubt; in
the second, the aim is the limitation of thought:

> "To bring us so salutary a determination, nothing
> can be more serviceable, than to be once thoroughly
> convinced of the force of the Pyrrhonian doubt,
> and of the impossibility, that anything, but the
> stronger power of natural instinct, could free us
> from it." (E 162)

To be aware of the stronger power of natural instinct
is tantamount to the awareness of the limitation of
the power of our thoughts. The stronger power of
natural instinct, stronger than the generalised
Pyrrhonian doubt about our power to think and to act,
is nothing but *nature* which determines us to act, to
reason and to believe. It is to go against this
natural instinct not to believe, while acting, in
the existence of objects. It is also against nature

to believe that thought can reach beyond concomitancy
and discover the real springs of nature. It is no
less against nature to try to remove sceptical conclusions concerning these two beliefs. Hence Cartesian confidence in the new science can be maintained
provided we exclude from the range of our intellectual
capacity "all distant and high enquiries" and leave

> "the more sublime topics to the embellishments of
> poets and orators, or to the arts of priests and
> politicians" (E 162).

If one equates Descartes' philosophy with scepticism
one should understand by it total scepticism about
the old science based on the projections of human
feeling on objects. Equally, if one equates Hume's
scepticism with mitigated scepticism then one should
understand by it total scepticism about the capacity
of reason to justify our belief in action and science
or alternatively to destroy our beliefs. Hume tried
to build a concept of knowledge which is so qualified
that it could not give any opportunity to its de-
tractors to attack it. He was certainly not trying
to defend the view that knowledge is possible, e.g.
that men can form a non-animistic picture of reality.
He took that for granted as Descartes did. Both of
them were more concerned with defining the new knowledge, the new physics, in familiar terms which would
not encourage esoteric interpretations of human intellectual powers and of nature. One could well imagine
Mathematics and Physics reaching their present advanced state without Descartes' Metaphysics, and certainly without Hume's *Treatise*. The precise nature
of their contribution is a problem which brings in
the question of the function of philosophy and also
the perplexing question of the nature of philosophical
innovation.

No problem is more obscure in the interpretation of
Cartesian philosophy than the importance he attributed to analysis. The *Meditations* has been seen as
the solution of a vast problem by analysis. Gilson
explains it as follows:

> "trouver les principes premiers de la physique.
> Celui qui veut procéder synthétiquement part des

principes les plus abstraits et les plus uni-
versels, dont il ne tire que des conclusions
verbales (scolastique); celui qui veut procéder
analytiquement cherche l'objet particulier le
plus simple et le plus aisé a connaître (*Cogito*),
qui lui livre du premier coup l'essence de l'âme
et, par conséquent, la distinction de l'âme et
du corps, principe de la physique cartésienne de
l'étendue et du mouvement." (*Discours* p. 189)[9]

Besides, Descartes adds, the analytical method shows
the true way by which a thing was discovered. This
notion of discovery and of invention in philosophical
matters will concern us specifically in the next two
chapters where we shall try to explore how Descartes
did innovate in questions like the nature of mind,
matter and knowledge. So far as knowledge is in
question and its relation to scepticism and certainty
we would like to draw attention to the difference
between the relation scepticism - knowledge in the
Meditations and the same relation in the post-Cartesian
period. We are not alluding to the novelty of the
Cartesian methodic doubt, but rather to the plaus-
ibility that the notion of knowledge Descartes was
working with is not longer the same when Descartes
finished his *Meditations*. Knowledge did not have the
same problematical character in pre-Cartesian philosophy as it will have in its post-Cartesian period.
It is appealing to see the whole of the history of
philosophy as the history of scepticism and of the
correlated quest for certainty. It places philosophy
categorically in a very close relation to science,
it does not sever its relation to religion, and it
obviously stresses the practical import of philosophy
in relation to legal and moral certainty. In Descartes'
eyes knowledge before the new physics was simply no
knowledge, his scepticism of the view that

"gravity carried bodies towards the centre of the
earth as if it contained some knowledge of this
centre within it." (HR II 55)

could not be properly called scepticism. Descartes
considered such a statement as false and absurd.

When later philosophers will debate problems of know-

ledge on the background of Cartesian dualism both
the notion of scepticism and of knowledge had already
changed their meaning. It seems that the real problem which tormented the young Descartes was: How
could the familiar though false picture of the universe which scholastic philosophy offered be replaced
by the new but unfamiliar picture of the new physics?
In *Le Monde* he tried the direct method by saying
bluntly what natural phenomena are not like; in the
first paragraph of the opening chapter he writes:

> "Me proposant de traiter ici de la lumière, la
> première chose dont je veux vous avertir est qu'il
> peut y avoir de la différence entre le sentiment
> que nous en avons, c'est-à-dire l'idée qui s'en
> forme en notre imagination par l'entremise de nos
> yeux, et ce qui est dans les objets qui produit
> en nous ce sentiment, c'est-à-dire ce qui est
> dans la flamme ou dans le Soleil, qui s'appelle
> du nom de Lumière." (Alquié I 315).

At the end of the chapter he nevertheless calms his
readers by saying that he does not want them to
believe absolutely that light in objects is different from light in the eyes but only

> "Afin que vous en doutiez, et que, vous gardant
> d'être préoccupé du contraire, vous puissiez
> maintenant mieux examiner avec moi ce qui en
> est." (319)

The explanation usually given for Descartes' not
having published his book on Physics, *Le Monde*, is
that he had just heard of the condemnation of Galileo
and therefore decided to present his physics through
his metaphysics. If in *Le Monde* he is suggesting
doubt and not absolute belief in the new scientific
explanation of the causes of light, in the *Meditations*
he will induce in his reader a sceptical attitude by
giving himself as an example of one who has taken
the "medicine" of doubt and come out cured. But
there is more than personal example in this so-called
analytical mode of presentation; there is the awareness that more than simple and straightforward doubt
is needed to bend the mind towards the new science.
It is not the case that sometimes a sentiment is
caused by a sentiment of the same nature and which

exists in the object and sometimes another sentiment
is caused by something radically different in the
object. In a word he needed the doctrine: qualities
are not in the objects, they are perceptions in the
mind. But whereas the scholastic view of nature
was familiar, though inclining to some laziness in
the mind, the new picture demanded an unfamiliar
view of nature. It is debatable whether Descartes
has really made us familiar with our mind; what is
not debatable is that we are now familiar with the
picture of the universe as totally devoid of sentiment. We are ready to accept the most extravagant
achievements of science without attributing any
supernatural power to scientists. And, if occultism
of any kind manifests itself in our contemporary
western society, it is often linked with some theory
of the human mind.

Descartes has succeeded in making us, through of
course all the philosophers who succeeded him, and
mainly through the British Empiricists, *nearly* absolutely familiar with our mind - a transparent mind.
In his review of Williams' book on *Descartes*, Anthony
Kenny repeats the thesis that the *official theory* of
mind is Cartesian:

> "Even today Descartes' concept of mind governs
> the thinking of many philosophers, whether or
> not they theoretically accept the criticisms of
> Kant and Wittgenstein: and it is the dominant
> one among the intellectually sophisticated people
> who are not professionally trained in philosophy."[10]

By what means did he introduce this official theory?
How did he succeed? Did he use a rhetorical device
available to him through some ambiguity in the
grammar of our language? In the following chapter
we shall examine the question whether Descartes
used rhetoric in order to induce his readers to
accept his theory of mind.

Notes

1. Richard A. Watson, *The Downfall of Cartesianism 1673-1712*, Martinus Nijhoff, The Hague, 1966, p. 146.

2. Gilbert Ryle, *The Concept of Mind*, Hutchinson's University Library, London, 1949, p. 11.

3. Robert Lenoble, *Mersenne ou la naissance du mécanisme* Paris, J. Vrin, 1943.

4. See Jonathan Rée, *Descartes*, Allen Lane, London, 1974.

5. *The Philosophical Works of Descartes*, 2 volumes, ed. and trans. Elisabeth S. Haldane and J.R.T. Ross, Cambridge University Press, 1911-12; 1934. Referred to as HR.

6. Étienne Gilson, *Études sur le rôle de la pensée médiévale dans la formation du système Cartésien*, Paris, J.Vrin, 1951, p.186.

7. Descartes, *Oeuvres Philosophiques*, 3 tomes, édition de F. Alquié, Garnier Frères, Paris, 1963-1973.

8. Henri Gouhier, *La Pensée Metaphysique de Descartes*, Paris, J. Vrin. 1962, p.33.

9. Etienne Gilson, *Discours de la Méthode: Texte et Commentaire*, cinquième édition, Paris, J.Vrin, 1976.

10. Anthony Kenny, rev. of *Descartes: The project of Pure Enquiry*, by Bernard Williams, *The Times Higher Educational Supplement*, 14 August 1978, p. 18.

CHAPTER III
Philosophy and Rhetoric

Language as a signifying activity is well illustrated by the new use Descartes made of the term
"idea". It would be impossible for Wittgenstein
to condemn the new usage introduced by Descartes
by pointing out that the term "idea" has no reference
since such a condemnation would be tantamount to a
return to a referential theory of meaning. Descartes'
theory of language as seen by semanticists of the
Wittgensteinian school is considered as the simple
prolongation of the Aristotelian conception of language. Language according to Aristotle is not a
power but a transcription of a series of concepts.
Cartesian ideas are invented items in the mind to
which words must correspond in order to have meaning.

However, if the term "idea" has been invented by
Descartes and is responsible for our misunderstanding
of our linguistic activity and further if we cannot
eradicate this usage by pointing to the fact that
nothing corresponds to such a term, the only way
left to us is to unveil the rhetorical device used
by Descartes:

> "How does the philosophical problem about mental
> processes and states and about behaviourism arise?
> The first step is the one that altogether escapes
> notice. We talk of processes and states and
> leave their nature undecided. Sometimes perhaps
> we shall know more about them - we think. But
> that is just what commits us to a particular way
> of looking at the matter. For we have a definite
> concept of what it means to learn to know a pro-
> cess better. (The decisive movement of the con-
> juring-trick has been made, and it was the very
> one that we thought quite innocent.)"[1]

Ideas in terms of which mental processes and states
are usually explained were left thus, according to

Wittgenstein, unexplained even though Cartesians
deluded themselves that they were characterising
them negatively: ideas are not objects. In a word,
ideas were assumed as existents and all Cartesians
including the Empiricists subscribed to what Arnauld
and Nicole wrote in their *Logique* (1662):

> "Le mot d'idée est du nombre de ceux qui sont si
> clairs- qu'on ne les peut expliquer par d'autres
> parce qu'il n'en a point de plus clairs et de plus
> simples."[2]

Moreover, most of the philosophers who started using
the term "idea" were perfectly aware that they were
using it in a new way, they were aware that it consisted in a linguistic invention. The latter could
not have been a symbolic innovation. Cartesian philosophy is opposed to any kind of symbolism. Matter
being reduced to extension and material changes to
motion, the new physics rejects the possibility that
objects could be symbols; things have no meaning
except what they are. And yet, as it has been repeatedly observed, Descartes' style is full of imagery, even in his most abstract and metaphysical
works. In his interesting contribution to the Cahiers
de Royaumont II (Paris, Ed. de Minuit, 1957), Th.
Spoerri: *La puissance métaphorique de Descartes,* has noted
that almost all of Descartes' images fall under three
themes: the road, the house, and the machine. These
rhetorical devices are very often of the nature of
illustrations, by way of comparison. There is not
in Descartes' imagery anything to complement what
he says in his non-figurative style. Could it have
been otherwise? Had not Descartes already in the
Regulae condemned Dialectics itself and relegated it
to the realm of Rhetoric?

> "It may perhaps strike some with surprise that
> here, where we are discussing how to improve our
> power of deducing one truth from another, we have
> omitted all the precepts of the dialecticians, by
> which they think to control the human reason...
> But to say a few words more, that it may appear
> still more evident that this style of arguments
> contributed nothing at all to the discovery of
> truth, we must note that the Dialecticians are

unable to devise any syllogism which has a true
conclusion, unless they have first secured the
material out of which to construct it, i.e. unless
they have already ascertained the very truth
which is deduced in the syllogism. Whence it is
clear that from a formula of this kind they can
gather nothing that is new, and hence the ordinary Dialectic is quite valueless for those who
desire to investigate the truth of things. Its
only possible use is to serve to explain at times
more easily to others the truths we have already
ascertained; hence it should be transferred from
Philosophy to Rhetoric." (HR I 32-33)

By one stroke traditional logic itself is excluded
from philosophy and assimilated to rhetoric which
has nothing to do with the search for truth. Even
if Thomas Sprat in his *History of The Royal Society* does
not make any reference to Descartes, only to Bacon,
it can be presumed that his readers must have viewed
Descartes' style as embodying most if not all Sprat's
stylistic recommendations which consist in a

"constant resolution, to reject all the amplifi-
cations, digressions, and swellings of style; to
return back to the primitive purity, and short-
ness, when men deliver'd so many things, almost
in an equal number of words."[3]

Who among the philosopher - scientists, more than
Descartes, could have achieved in his writings the
concise, non-figurative, mathematical, plain style?
And Descartes gives his final verdict against Rhetoric in the *Discourse* where he declares that order
and method are the best means for persuasion:

"Those who have the strongest power of reasoning,
and who most skilfully arrange their thoughts in
order to render them clear and intelligible, have
the best power of persuasion even if they can
but speak the language of Lower Brittany and have
never learned Rhetoric." (HR I 85)

There is however in the *Reply to Objections VI* a passage
where Descartes contrasts conviction and persuasion

and seems to be ready to complement his logical and
metaphysical demonstrations by rhetorical persuasion.
His lack of persuasion concerned the proof of the
distinction mind-body. Henri Gouhier in *La Pensée
Métaphysique de Descartes* has devoted a whole chapter
to what he calls "La résistance au vrai dans une
philosophie sans rhétorique." It would be too much
to expect from Gouhier to call his chapter, where
he examines the possibility that Descartes might
have resorted to rhetoric, otherwise than he did.
No, Descartes could not have taken refuge in rhetorical persuasion because rhetoric, besides being
concerned with words only, was penetrated by the
bad philosophy. It is not very difficult to grasp
in what sense scholastic philosophy was intermingled
with rhetoric. The kind of rhetoric taught, for
instance, at la Flèche, was a variant of an Aristotelian rhetoric with the accretions and commentaries
by Cicero and Quintillian published in a book by
Cyprien Soarez in 1596. In the Aristotelian sense
Rhetoric and Dialectic are both contrasted with
Science. While the latter starts from true premisses,
the former starts from probable premisses. Rhetorical
arguments must have a minimum grounding in Reason
in order to achieve persuasion. Knowledge or familiarity with the psychology of the auditor is not
enough. Textbooks of Dialectic and Rhetoric contain
numerous examples drawn from philosophy. Thus the
reader of the *Logique de Port Royal*, in the seventeenth
and eighteenth century, expects to find examples
which illustrate the Section dealing with *The Method*
(inspired mainly by Descartes' *Regulea*) and a modern
reader might be surprised to read that the examples
are again the same that Descartes used in *Le Monde*
(physics), in the *Discourse* and the *Meditations*, that
is in an *Introduction to Physics* and in the *Foundations
of Physics*.

The question is whether Gouhier is right when he
takes the view that rhetoric could not be used by
Descartes because the examples of probable truth
were drawn from Scholastic philosophy. It would not
have been an extraordinary intellectual achievement
had Descartes separated the Method of Rhetoric from
its examples, and replaced them by others from his

Dioptrics. So it must have been for other reasons
that he rejected both Dialectic and classical Rhetoric. Some of the reasons as we noted above, were
that eloquence is not teachable, it is a gift of
Nature, of God, and that in the pursuit of truth
order and clarity are eloquence. In either case it
is useless for a philosopher to learn eloquence.
But of course, when we strip rhetoric from its standard philosophical examples, we are left with the
sheer power of words and their effects on the list-
ener or reader. So we must conclude that Gouhier
is wrong when he writes that Descartes separates
rhetoric from philosophy because it studies reason in
abstraction of the sciences which show reason in
action.

It is sometimes argued that in Descartes' philosophy
as well as in others of the seventeenth century on-
ward, the new notion of evidence excluded any even-
tual revival of rhetoric. Now, this notion of evidence included both what we call evidence and what
we call arguments confirming or disqualifying the
evidence. To say that if the true is evident it
cannot impose itself except by the very nature of
the evidence (without any recourse to rhetoric) is
to overlook the close connexion between evidence
and reason. The notion of evidence whether in the
context of Protestant personal evidence or in the
context of scientific evidence included in it a new
concept of reason, a new type of argument, which
says that persuasion is the result of truth on others
as on the speaker or writer who utters this truth.
But if truth persuades how could Descartes himself
tell the authors of the Sixth Objections that he was
not persuaded by his own logical and metaphysical
proof of the distinction mind-body?

> "When first the reasons expounded in these Med-
> itations had led me to infer that the human mind
> was really distinct from the body and was more
> easily known than it, and so on, what compelled
> me to assent to this was that I found nothing in
> these arguments which was not coherent nor derived
> from highly evident principles according to the
> rules of Logic. But I confess that I was not
> thereby wholly persuaded, and that I had almost

the same experience as the Astronomers, who,
after many proofs had convinced them that the
Sun was many times larger than the Earth, could
not prevail upon themselves to forgo judging that
it was smaller than the Earth when they viewed
it with their eyes." (HR II 253)

Rather than leading Descartes' commentators to the
hypothesis that Descartes devised a rhetoric of his
own which would persuade himself and others, this
confession which Descartes makes in his answer to
the Sixth Objections, led them into the study of
the psychology presupposed by Aristotelian physics.
Thus, philosophy does not consist only in detecting
error and seeing the truth, it demands a break with
our childhood habits. Otherwise, authentic evidence
would never have any hold on us. Ultimately the
confession is interpreted as a reminder of Descartes'
intellectual rationalism, his distrust of the senses,
which he expresses very often in his writings as for
instance in Part IV of the *Discourse*:

> "What causes many, however, to persuade themselves
> that there is difficulty in knowing this truth,
> and even in knowing the nature of their soul, is
> the fact that they never raise their minds above
> the things of sense, or that they are so accus-
> tomed to consider nothing excepting by imagining
> it, which is a mode of thought specially adapted
> to material objects, that all that is not capable
> of being imagined appears to them not to be intel-
> ligible at all." (HR I 104)

There is, therefore, a psychology based on habits
acquired during childhood which is the same as that
of the scholastic reader of Descartes' *Meditations*,
and you could call it the psychology presupposed by
scholastic physics. Nobody should read the *Meditations*,
Descartes writes in the Preface, unless he is ready
to meditate with him seriously, and try to comprehend the order and connexions of his reasonings. A
mind which has been stunted by error and which wants
to conquer truth is like a soul which wants to reform
itself by meditating on the true nature of God. In
both cases a strict discipline is required on the

arduous way towards the truth. The discipline is
indispensable not only in the effort required for
the methodic doubt but also during the intervals
which must be used to reflect on what has been
previously achieved. The language of the *Meditations*
does not contain some hidden force (a rhetoric)
which absolves the reader from making the efforts
he is required to make. The power of the *Meditations*
consists only in the order of the arguments. Nevertheless, it would be difficult to contend that the
learned priest, author of the First Objections, did
not follow carefully the reasons in their order.
Far from it, not only did he carefully analyse the
Cartesian argument on the proof of the existence of
God but he also noticed very clearly and distinctly
that Descartes is using the term "idea" in a sense
different from the usual accepted philsophical
meaning:

> *"But here I am forced to stop a little, to avoid excessive
> exhaustion; for already my mind fluctuates like the Euripus
> with its changing tides. Now I consent, now I deny: I
> approve and once more disapprove. To disagree with the
> champion of this theory I do not care, agree with him I
> cannot. But, pray, what sort of cause must an idea have?
> or, tell me, what is an idea? It is the thing thought of
> itself in so far as that is 'objectively' in the under-
> standing. But explain what 'to be objectively in the
> understanding' is. As I was taught, it is the determin-
> ation of an act of the mind by a modification due to an
> object; but this is a merely external attribute of the
> thing and nothing belonging to its reality. For, as 'being
> seen' is merely the direction of the act of vision towards
> the percipient so 'being thought' or 'being objectively in
> the understanding' is merely a standing still of our thought
> within itself and ending there, which can occur whether
> the thing is active or passive, indeed though it is even
> non-existent. Hence, why should I ask for a cause of that
> which is nothing actual, which is a mere name, a nonen-
> tity."* [2] *(HR II 2)*

As Gilson explains it in his Texts et Commentaire
of *Discours de la Méthode*, Caterus could not see why
Descartes is positing a reality of our representation
in addition to a) the reality of the object, b) the
reality of the intellect, c) the reality of the

intellectual act. In a word: our knowledge, in
scholastic philosophy, is not a knowledge of ideas,
it is a knowledge of things, and the objects of
knowledge are the things themselves. Gilson explains:

> "Toute différente est la position adoptée par
> Descartes. Au lieu de partir, comme la scolas-
> tique, du contact entre la pensée et l'objet,
> d'ou naît le concept, il part le la pensée pure,
> avec le *cogito*. Dès lors, la ressemblance entre
> le concept et l'objet, que la Scholastique trouve
> déjà expliquée par l'objet lui - même dès le
> premier moment ou elle le constate, est encore
> inexpliquée pour Descartes, et ne peut même être
> que postulée par lui lorsqu'il la rencontre.
> Bien loin, en effet, de pouvoir en rendre raison
> par l'objet, c'est sur elle qu'il doit nécess-
> airement s'appuyer pour poser cet objet; il
> affirmera donc, contrairement à l'École, que 'du
> connaître à l'être la conséquence est bonne'
> (VII al *Resp.*, t. VII, p. 520, 1.5), et se placera
> dans les conditions requises pour que le passage
> de l'idée à l'être puisse légitimement s'effec-
> tuer."[4]

Instead of the elaborate conceptual apparatus used to
describe our intellectual power by Scholastic philosophy, Descartes was prescribing a reduced and very
simple apparatus. But, this reduction implied, as
Gilson explains, a total change in our conception
of knowledge. It seems therefore that neither the
arguments nor the meditation over the intent of the
argument could separately or even together persuade
a scholastic reader like Caterus. Those already persuaded of the need for a new concept of knowledge,
Gassendi, Marsenne and Hobbes, queried the utility
of the new metaphysical foundations of physics. The
new Cartesian way of ideas did not persuade them
either. The new physics carried within itself the
power to convince and persuade, at least those who
knew how utterly barren Aristotelian physics was.

For the layman who could not judge either way in so
far as science is concerned, the new way of ideas
was even stranger than for the Scholastic philosopher.

Joseph Glanvill in his *Vanity of Dogmatizing* gives a
vivid picture of the popular reaction to the conclusion of science that heat, colour and sound are
not in the objects but in the mind:

> "Secondly the *best Philosophy* (the deserved Title
> of the *Cartesian*) derives all sensitive perceptions
> from *Motion*, and corporal impress; some account of
> which we have above given.... So that what we
> term *heat* and *cold*, and other qualities, are not
> properly according to *Philosophical* rigour in the
> Bodies, their Efficients: but are rather *Names*
> expressing our *passions;* ... This I conceive to
> be an *Hypothesis*, well worthy a rational belief:
> and yet it is so abhorrent from the Vulgar, that
> they would assoon believe *Anaxagoras*, that *snow is
> black*, as him that should affirm it is not *white*;
> ..." (V 87-89)

In this passage Glanvill, a member of the Royal
Society, gives the best expression of what Descartes
meant by the habits we acquire during our childhood,
habits concerning the projection of whatever we feel
on external objects. There is no need for argument
to show that the *Meditations* or even the *Discourse*
were not meant for the layman. From the question
concerning how Descartes could persuade his readers,
we were led to the question concerning the type of
readers to whom the *Meditations* were addressed. For
the Scholastic reader the reality of the idea was
a gratuitous reification, for the disciple of Galileo,
it was more often than not superfluous, and for the
layman it was abhorrent.

There are some philosophers who think that the Cartesian picture of man as a thinking substance to
which mechanical laws do not apply was the deter-
mining factor for its acceptance and its gradual
transformation into the official theory of the dualistic nature of man. As a result of the new physics,
at the end of the sixteenth century and the beginning
of the seventeenth century, the world was no longer
the familiar world we can see, feel, smell, and hear,
but an alien extended matter in motion completely
devoid of any human sentiment. If we accept such

an interpretation then it would be the case that
the Cartesian text itself, with its arguments and
its style was nothing in comparison with the simple
message which Descartes conveyed: man is not a
machine.

Upon the last interpretation of Cartesian dualism,
it is not this form of style, or that form of reasoning which persuaded and convinced Descartes'
readers. It is rather the picture of man totally
unlike the vast clockwork - the universe, which
comforted him and his readers.

There is still, however, the possibility that the
analytic method of presentation in the *Meditations*
is responsible for their persuasive power. Descartes
believed that analysis shows the true way by which
something has been methodically invented. We are
asked to assent to some view by being shown how
the writer himself builds up his arguments leading
to this view. Synthesis, writes Descartes, unlike
analysis, does not give the reader's mind the satisfaction of being taught the method by which the
theory was invented. Descartes believed in analysis
both as an inventor and as a teacher, and advanced
the hypothesis that the ancient geometers of Greece
had suppressed the knowledge of this method:

> "Possibly they acted, just as many inventors are
> known to have done in the case of their discov-
> eries, i.e. they feared that their method being
> so easy and simple would become cheapened on
> being divulged, and they preferred to exhibit
> in its place certain barren truths, deductively
> demonstrated which show enough of ingenuity, as
> the results of their arts, in order to win from
> us our admiration for these achievements, rather
> than disclose to us the method itself which
> would have wholly annulled the admiration
> accorded." (HR I 12)

In the sythetic version of the *Meditations* the method
of doubt is reduced to a postulate which does not
have the existential dimension or the therapeutic
effect of the methodic doubt in its itinerary. It

is not enough to be told, as we are by Descartes in the *Discourse*, of his intention to re-examine all the opinions he held until he began his Meditations, in order to be persuaded of the distinction between soul and body. The *Discourse* does not exhibit the analytic method but it contains some allusion that the methodic doubt has been used.

Nevertheless, since the mere assurance that the analytic method is the method of invention in geometry does not carry us automatically to the same assurance that the method is equally successful in metaphysics, we are left with the hypothesis that the main instrument of persuasion in the *Meditations* is the methodic doubt. In the *Reply to Objections VI*, however, Descartes confides that even after the methodic doubt and the logical and metaphysical demonstrations which followed, he was convinced but not persuaded. So we are back again to where we started. It is not enough to doubt methodically, it is not enough to counter the habits of childhood by systematic doubt, it is not enough to follow step by step the arguments leading from the *Cogito* to the final conclusion of the Sixth Meditation, in order to be persuaded of the truth of this conclusion. Something much more prosaic was needed in order to persuade Descartes about his metaphysical and logical demonstrations: to remember in what terms he construed Aristotelian physics. It is there that the real invention occurs.

Before we deal with the solution of Descartes' doubts about his proof of the distinction between mind and body as he relates this solution in his *Reply to Objections VI*, we have to ask ourselves some further questions about the nature of rhetoric.

Rhetoric can be equated, first with the power which language has over our sentiments and passions and even our reasoning. Secondly, rhetoric is an attempt to explain the mechanism by which words have this power. From the fact that Descartes discards any form of expression which does not address itself to reason one could easily conclude, as many have

done, that Descartes' writings do not contain any
rhetoric: there is no trace in the *Meditations* for
instance, of any appeal to feeling. The force of
the Cartesian arguments is derived solely from the
natural light of reason. One could of course stress
the metaphorical character of Cartesian expressions
such as "natural light", "clear and distinct ideas",
"the distinct vision by mind", and yet these expressions derive their force from the purely intellectual
nature of reason and not the other way round. Descartes' arguments would remain intact without his
figurative way of describing ideas and mind.

But could Descartes have anything to do with rhetoric
as a theory? In his *Letter to Father Dinet,* Descartes
rejects the accusation that it is because youth is
imbued with the principles of his philosophy that
they cannot understand any longer the terminology
used by Scholastic philosophers:

"As though it were a necessity that philosophy,
which is only instituted for the knowledge of
the truth, should teach certain terms of which
it itself has no need! Why does he not condemn
grammar and rhetoric, because it is rather their
function to treat of words, while yet they are
so much opposed to the teaching of those scholastic terms that they reject them as barbarous?
Were he therefore to complain that *by them youth
is turned away from the study of the true philosophy,
and prevented from reaching the fullness of erudition,*
there would be no reason for laughing at him
more than when he says the same of our philosophy;
for it is not from it, but from the writings of
those who make use of these terms that we should
expect their explanation." (HR II 371)

It is therefore clear from the above quotation that
rhetoric as a study of words *qua* words, did take its
distance from scholastic philosophy and was not
"penetrated by the wrong philosophy" as Henri Gouhier
maintains in his book *La Pensée Métaphysique de Descartes.*
Apparently Descartes must have read books on Rhetoric
in which readers were advised to abstain from using
"barbarous" expressions like "sympathy", "antipathy",

and other similar obscure terms. Descartes, however, does not think that a "technical wordy" approach to the philosophical terminology of the Schools could have any effect on the validity of such a philosophy. It is as ridiculous to attack Cartesian philosophy because it abstains from using scholastic terminoloy as it is to blame rhetoric for its criticism of scholastic terminology. If this scholastic terminology is fading away then the only people to blame are those who use it in their philosophy and pretend that they can discover the truth with its help. Rhetoric thus appears to be, philosophically speaking, a neutral discipline which cannot constitute by itself any source in the discovery of truth.

The Wittgensteinian analysis of the notion of language presupposed by Cartesianism is thus corroborated by Descartes himself: both Language and the study of Language (rhetoric and grammar) are inert and do not partake, in any way, in our real intellectual power. Descartes' attitude to language is even more specifically expressed in his often quoted Letter to Mersenne of the 20th of November 1629 where he comments on the feasibility and utility of a Universal language.

"Au reste, je trouve qu'on pourrait ajouter à ceci une invention, tant pour composer les mots primitifs de cette langue que pour leurs caractères; en sorte qu'elle pourrait être enseignée en fort peu de temps, et ce par le moyen de l'ordre, c'est-à-dire, établissant un ordre entre toutes les pensées qui peuvent entrer en l'esprit humain, de même qu'il y en a un naturellement établi entre les nombres; et comme on peut apprendre en un jour à nommer tous les nombres jusques à l'infini, et à les écrire en une langue inconnue, qui sont toutefois une infinité de mots différents, qu'on pût faire le même de tous les autres choses qui tombent en l'esprit des hommes."

In other words a Universal language depends on the true philosophy and Descartes is hopeful concerning such a language if

"... si quelqu'un avait bien expliqué quelles sont les idées simples qui sont en l'imagination des

hommes, desquelles se compose tout ce qu'ils
pensent, et que cela fût reçu par tout le
monde..." (Alquié I 230, 231)

Rhetoric and grammar are indeed excluded from philosophy not because they are the vehicle of the wrong
philosophy but solely because language is a purely
arbitrary institution, a human convention, absolutely
dependent on the thoughts and ideas which were previously in the mind. The power of words is derived
from the fact that they stand for ideas. Consequently it is natural to conclude that Descartes
could not and did not have any interest in Rhetoric
as a theoretical subject which explores the power
of words, since anyway he refused any power to words
qua words.

It might be the case that we must add a third meaning to Rhetoric besides the traditional practical
and theoretical meanings: the introduction in the
usage of language of a new term of expression which
adds to the language a power it lacked hitherto.
As an illustration of what we intend by this third
meaning of Rhetoric we can contrast the style in
which a thinker like Glanvill talks about our intellectual power and the style of Locke, to take one
of the earliest philosophers in England who used
the language of ideas. At the level of the description of our intellectual operations it is surprising
how simplifying is the use of the term "idea" whose
function could be compared to the function of the
variable in algebra for solving an arithmetical
problem. This is how Glanvill writes about sensation:

> "But besides those absurdities, that lie more
> deep, and are of a mysterious alloy; we are at
> a loss for a scientifical account even of our
> Senses, the most knowable of our faculties. Our
> eyes, that see other things, see not themselves:
> and those principal foundations of knowledge are
> themselves unknown." (V 27)

Glanvill was writing in 1661, and he became member
of the Royal Society a few years before Locke. He
was a disciple of More and a great admirer of

Descartes and yet, in spite of his acceptance of
Cartesian dualism he never uses the "transparent
language of ideas" in order to give an account of
perception in terms of mental entities. Glanvill
remains entangled with the problem of the interaction
between mind and body all the way through and never
assumes what the Cartesians assume, a direct acquaintance with our mental operations. He considers the
interaction between mind and body as mysterious and
hence sensation remains in a no man's land between
the physical and the mental and he asks:

> "But how is it, and by what Art doth the soul
> read that such and image or stroke in matter
> [whether that of her vehicle, or of the Brain,
> the case is the same] signifies such an object?
> Did we learn such an Alphabet in our Embryo-state?
> And how comes it to pass, that we are not aware
> of any such congenite apprehensions?" (V 30)

Contrary to Glanvill, Locke does not think that the
simple ideas of sense are defined by stating the
physical conditions of their manifestations. Since
Locke works consistently on the premiss that ideas
are dichotomically distinct from their causes, the
obscurity in the notion of interaction does not
prevent him from writing as follows about perception:

> "PERCEPTION, as it is the first faculty of the
> mind exercised about our ideas; so it is the first
> and simplest idea we have from reflection, and
> is by some called thinking in general."

Having already introduced the variable, the term
"idea", in the definition of perception, he goes on
to say:

> "What perception is, every one will know better
> by reflecting on what he does himself, when he
> sees, hears, feels, &c., or thinks, than by any
> discourse of mine. Whoever reflects on what
> passes in his own mind cannot miss it. And if
> he does not reflect, all the words in the world
> cannot make him have any notion of it." (Bk.II.
> ix. 1-2) [5]

It should be noted that both Glanvill and Locke
appeal to awareness and while Glanvill seems to be
groping to become aware of the notion of perception
by becoming aware of the mind's reading the physical
image in the brain, Locke is aware of the mental act
only. Were it not that Locke has already accepted
the Cartesian notion of idea as the material of
thinking and of knowledge he would not be capable
of discoursing so literally about the contents of
our minds.

Our comparison of the term "idea" with the algebraic
variable should be qualified: whereas when the mathematical problem is solved the variable disappears - at
least in the solution of simple arithmetical problems -
(and our inventory of numbers does not contain on
the occasion of the momentary introduction of the
variable, variables and numbers, but only numbers),
not only the ideas do not vanish after the explanation of philosophy but they seem to exist even
more certainly than the objects they represent.
Besides, the variable standing for an unknown number
could in no way be described as better known than
the number it stands for - at least in a straightforward meaning of "known". We cannot find in
Descartes' *Regulae* any hint that he wanted to apply
the analytic method to the human mind and its contents. Analysis of course starts with Descartes'
assumption that in all our everyday practice we
deal with objects and sentiments which by their
nature are composite. Science tries to reduce these
"composite natures" to "simple natures". The use of
variables is mainly meant to represent "simple natures" in the physical world; the use of analysis is
similarly centred on the transformation of a problem in physics or geometry into an algebraic problem and ultimately on its solution by solving the
equations in which the variables represent known
and unknown quantities.

Descartes mentions in Rule XII and XIII as an illustration of the method of analysis his approach to
the problem of magnetism. In Rule XII our observations and experience of the magnet are finally
explained by being equated to effects caused by the

intermixture of the simple natures such as motion,
figure and extension. In Rule XIII Descartes spec-
ifies in what sense his method of analysis resembles
the Dialecticians' syllogistic method: while the
latter assume, in teaching their doctrine of the
forms of syllogism, that the terms or matter of
their syllogisms are *known*, the Cartesian method
assumes only that the question to be solved should
be perfectly understood. It goes without saying
that in this seemingly innocent similarity and the
equally innocent difference, e.g. the initial assumption of something, and the distinction between
assuming knowledge and assuming understanding, lies
the fundamental difference of modern philosophy from
traditional Aristotelianism.

In Rule X Descartes has previously explained his
method as an inquiry into the solutions already found
by others. The Cartesian inquiry requires a sharp
distinction between knowledge and understanding:
understanding is not knowledge. In training ourselves to probe into the ways received knowledge
has been acquired, we train ourselves in the mental
discipline required for reaching new knowledge.
What is knowledge for the dialectician becomes a
problem to be solved for Descartes:

"Firstly, in every question there must be something of which we are ignorant; otherwise there
is no use asking the question. Secondly, this
very matter must be designated in some way or
other; otherwise there would be nothing to
determine us to investigate it rather than anything else. Thirdly, it can only be so designated
by the aid of something else which is already
known." (HR I 49)

If we compare the fundamental principle lying behind Rule XIII with the so-called Cartesian principle consisting in the search for absolute foundations of our knowledge, we would have to conclude
either that the quest for foundations is a later
development in Descartes' thought or that this
"quest" has been the product of later interpreters
of the Cartesian philosophy. In a language which

later will be adopted by the Empiricists, Decartes,
in Rule XII, in the enquiry relating the nature of
the magnet, dismisses as irrelevant any question
which is not within the range of our understanding:

> "Thus, if the question is, 'what is the nature
> of the magnet?' people like that at once prog-
> nosticate difficulty and toil in the inquiry,
> and dismissing from the mind every well-known
> fact, fasten on whatsoever is most difficult,
> vaguely hoping that by ranging over the fruitless
> field where multifarious causes lie, they will
> find something fresh."

The inquiry must start with the observations and
experience which are perfectly understood and end
in the knowledge of how these understood observations
and experience can be deduced from the simple natures:

> "This achieved, he can boldly assert that he has
> discovered the real nature of the magnet in so
> far as human intelligence and the given exper-
> imental observations can supply him with this
> knowledge." (HR I 47)

The interpretation of Descartes' philosophy as the
quest for the absolute foundations of knowledge is
naturally connected with the doctrine of ideas. How
did the inquiry into the right method of science
become an inquiry into the nature of mind is a question which will be clarified by answering the question how the inquiry into the nature, say, of the
magnet, can be solved by knowing the nature of mind.

Bearing in mind our comparison of the obscurity
inherent in the description of our mental powers
made by a thinker who does not use the terminology
of ideas, with the *clarity* of style achieved by all
the users of the term "idea", we are in a position
to ask whether this apparent clarity is the result
of a new introspective science of the mind or an
invented rhetoric to familiarise the readers with
the methods and achievements of the new science.
Descartes realised how difficult it would be for
readers not versed in mathematics and the new physics

to understand his reduction of problems of knowledge
to equations involving variables standing for known
and unknown entities. He is already aware of this
obstacle when in the Rule XIV he writes:

"My desire is that here I may find a reader who
is an eager student of Arithmetic and Geometry,
though indeed I should prefer him to have no
practice in these arts, rather than to be adept
after the ordinary standard." (HR I 57)

And it needs no argument to show that what Descartes
is after in this Rule is what we would now call the
logical foundations of mathematics, definitely something more abstract than mathematics.

The *Rules for the Direction of the Mind* appeared in print
only in 1701. However, some of its contents was used
in *The Port-Royal Logic* by Arnauld and Nicole which
appeared in 1664, long after the *Discourse* and the
Meditations had had their impact on European thought.
It is therefore safe to assume that this impact of
Descartes' philosophy was due primarily to his philosophical works rather than to his scientific or
logical works, like the *Regulae*, or *Le Monde* or even
the *Dioptrics*, the *Meteors* and the *Geometry*.

It could well be the case that Descartes' language
of ideas which was adopted by the Empiricists was
not at all meant as Prolegomena to the Science of
Mind but, paradoxically enough, as an effective
method to prevent mental problems from interfering
with the new concept of objectivity in nature. The
new way of ideas must have been conceived as the
best defence, the safest prophylactic measure against
the contamination of nature by the human soul. It
is not enough to advocate that nature is only motion
and does not contain human feelings, it is not even
enough to succeed in doing physics without substantial
forms and occult qualities. What is imperative is
to produce a theory of the human soul which is absolutely devoid of any mystery, otherwise the mystery
will be transferred to the object of knowledge. The
human soul is admittedly the instrument which makes
man a knowing animal. Obscurity in our vision of

the soul is bound to pass into our knowledge and
into the object of knowledge. In doing physics
without substantial forms we assume the separation
between mind and body. But assuming that mind is
distinct from body, not knowing what is mind would
not secure the distinction. Our childhood habits,
the old philosophy, the need for action will soon
make us forget the distinction between mind and body
and jeopardise the successful establishment of the
new scientific attitude. In order to "contain" the
inherited propulsion of the human mind to project
itself over the objects, our notion of mind must be
absolutely transparent so that it could be actually
dispensed with when knowledge is achieved. Voltaire
seems to be complaining against this over-simplied
picture of the human soul as solely a thinking thing:

> "Our Des Cartes, born to discover the Errors of
> Antiquity, and at the same time substitute his
> own; and hurried away by that systematic Spirit
> which throws a Cloud over the Minds of the great-
> est men, thought he has demonstrated that the
> Soul is the same Thing as Thought, in the same
> Manner as Matter, in his Opinion is the same as
> Extension."[6]

Voltaire contrasts Descartes' "romance of the soul"
with the history of it as given by Locke. Had we
not had the "romance" of the soul as entirely distinct
from matter could we have had later the "history"
of the soul *tout court?* The whole so-called historical method in the study of human understanding which
Locke uses is entirely based on the transparency of
the new term "idea". In it Descartes summarised his
new approach to science, to the extent that not only
our mind was reduced to a thinking thing, but all
our knowledge became a knowledge of ideas. In Descartes' mature philosophical writings ideas end by
becoming the only simple natures needed for scientific speculation. The introduction by Descartes of
the new usage of the term "idea" was not intended
primarily to simplify our view of the nature of mind,
although this simplification was considered by him
as the guarantee for his knowledge of nature.

In the end his view of the nature of mind encapsu-
lated his physics. So much so, that what was probably a rhetorical invention - the new usage of the
term "idea" - became the principle of all Descartes'
philosophy. As we shall see later, a hundred years
after Descartes wrote the *Discourse*, scientific positivism was still in need of the rhetoric of ideas
in order to counter not only the sceptical consequences of Aristotelianism but also those of Cartesianism itself. Hume, according to our interpretation, will follow Descartes in reducing the soul
to thoughts; he will go further, and generalise the
theory of ideas to apply to *all* the qualities found
in bodies and even to the causal connexions between
bodies. Philosophical books are more often than not
full of all sorts of linguistic innovations, most
of them condemned to be used mainly, if not only,
by their inventors. It seems safe to assume that
the force wielded by any new term invented by a
philosopher cannot lie in itself, not even in the
use made of it. The power, the clarity, of a new
expression must have their origin in other linguistic
usages which eventually find in the new invented
expression a manner of uniting them and reinforcing
them.

Notes

1. Ludwig Wittgenstein, *Philosophical Investigations*,
   trans. J.E.M. Anscombe, second edition, Blackwell,
   Oxford, 1968, p.103e, par. 308.

2. Antoine Arnauld et Pierre Nicole, *La Logique ou
   l'Art de Penser*, Introduction de Louis Marin,
   Flammarion, 1970, p. 65.

3. *The History of the Royal Society, for the Improving of
   Natural Knowledge*. By Tho. Sprat, D.D., London,
   1702, sect. XX, p.113.

4. Étienne Gilson, *Discours de la Méthode: Texte et Commentaire*, cinquiéme édition, Paris, J. Vrin, 1976, p.322.

5. John Locke, *An Essay Concerning Human Understanding*, (1690), ed. A.C. Fraser, two volumes, Dover Publications, New York, 1959, I,p. 183.

6. Voltaire, *Letters Concerning the English Nation*, London, 1733, p. 97.

CHAPTER IV
Descartes' Use of the Term "Idea"

As hinted already in the preceding chapter, when
Descartes found himself unpersuaded following his
logical and metaphysical proof of the distinction
between mind and body, he again persuaded himself
by going back to the language of *Le Monde*. However,
before relating in full the text of his *Reply to
Objections VI*, it would be useful to recall the metaphysical form of the proof. Aware as he was that
no philosophy could ever be offered as an alternative to the Aristotelian unless it followed the
deductive model of starting from first principles,
Descartes translated his new philosophy of science
into the Aristotelian language of principles, God,
First cause, substances, and knowledge. In his own
words,

> "We must begin with the-investigation of these
> first causes, i.e. of the Principles. It is also
> necessary that these Principles should have two
> conditions attached to them: first of all they
> should be so clear and evident that the mind of
> man cannot doubt their truth when it attentively
> applies itself to consider them: in the second
> place it is on them that the knowledge of other
> things depends, so that the Principles can be
> known without these last, but the other things
> cannot reciprocally be known without the Prin-
> ciples. We must accordingly try to so deduce
> from these Principles the knowledge of the things
> that depend on them, that there shall be nothing
> in the whole series of the deductions made from
> them which shall not be perfectly manifest." (HR
> I 204)

Descartes, in the "Author's Letter to the Translator" of the *Principles of Philosophy* (from which the
above quotation is taken), alludes to his other
writings, *Of Meteors, Of the Dioptric, Of Geometry,* and
of course to the first part of the *Discourse,* and

81

stresses how he explained his inventions and others'
in Logic, Geometry, Astronomy, and Optics, and how
his discoveries in Physics and Mathematics are due
to his new philosophy. As for the *Meditations*, Descartes explains that his intention in writing them
was to make it *easier* for his readers to grasp the
assumptions, the metaphysical foundations of his new
mathematics, logic, and science.

Nevertheless, it seems that what was meant to be
helpful to others in understanding the assumptions
of the new science left Descartes still unpersuaded.
The habits obtained in childhood, the instruction
received in school, the needs of action, all of them
contributed to Descartes' reluctance to acquiesce
to the translation of his physics into the language
of metaphysics:

> "But since these opinions differed greatly from
> the beliefs which I had previously possessed
> respecting the same things, I began to reflect
> as to what has caused me to believe otherwise
> before ..." (HR II 254)

The difficulty in interpreting what Descartes means
in his *Reply to Objections VI* can be summed up as
follows: is it the bare distinction between mind
and body assumed but not "demonstrated" in Descartes'
practice of the new physics (see *Le Monde*) which
allows the old beliefs to reign in his mind or is
it that in spite of logical and metaphysical "demonstrations" he is under the sway of his childhood
beliefs? Descartes' answer is quite clear, and
stresses the hold of the old beliefs in spite of
the fact

> "that I found nothing in these arguments which
> was not coherent nor derived from highly evident
> principles according to the rules of Logic." (HR
> II 253)

And despite this most commentators have found nothing
but more "logical and metaphysical" arguments in
Descartes' reply to his unconvinced and unpersuaded
Objectors.

Descartes' further arguments are nothing more than
a description of the way he went along discarding all
the substantial forms, one after the other, in his
scientific discoveries and explanations of these
discoveries:

> "For since I conceived gravity, for example, in
> the fashion of a real quality of a certain order,
> which inhered in solid bodies, although I called
> it a *quality*, in so far as I referred it to the
> bodies in which it inhered, yet because I added
> the epithet *real*, I thought in truth that it was
> a substance; just as clothing regarded by itself
> is a substance, although when referred to the
> man whom it clothes it is a quality." (H II 254)

As the mind was similarly regarded as a quality of
the body, this, explains Descartes, led him to conceive of the "real qualities" of bodies in terms
of "mental qualities":

> "But the chief sign that my idea of gravity was
> derived from that which I had of the mind, is
> that I thought that gravity carried bodies towards
> the centre of the earth as if it contained some
> knowledge of this centre within it." (HR II 255)

So motion was interpreted in terms of human actions
which assume knowledge in the object:

> "For it could not act as it did without knowledge,
> nor can there be knowledge except in the mind."

And this animistic interpretation of material motion
was coupled with the usual material characteristics
which, in no way, could be attributed to mind, such
as divisibility and measurability. Only when
Descartes uses his new *Rule of ideas* could he be released from his doubts:

> "But after I had noted these things with suffic-
> ient care, and had accurately distinguished the
> idea of mind from the ideas of body and corporeal
> movement, and had discovered that all my previous
> ideas of real qualities or substantial forms had
> been composed or manufactured by me out of the

former set of ideas, I easily released myself
from all the doubts that are here advanced." (HR
II 255)

But this is nearly word by word a paraphrase of the
opening paragraph of *Le Monde* already quoted by us
and in which Descartes states clearly that no knowledge about the causes of light could be reached
unless we cease to assume that there is no difference between the sentiment or idea of light and
the cause of light in the object. By returning to
the practice of modern physics Descartes is again
aware that he no longer uses the language of "real
qualities and substantial forms" and *he uses instead
the language of ideas*. When in his *Principles of Philosophy*
Descartes recapitulates at the end of Part I the
principal causes of error, he mentions the prejudices
of childhood, the impossibility of forgetting these
prejudices, the difficulty of applying our attention
to intellectual matters and he ends:

> *"The fourth cause is that we attach our concepts to words
> which do not accurately answer to reality."* (HR I 212)

And the typical example of this is the previously
quoted passage where he relates how he called gravity
a quality and then added to it "the epithet *real*".
In sum, all our difficulties in understanding the
new physics come ultimately from our linguistic
habits which perpetuate the prejudices of childhood,
implant these prejudices in our memory, and prevent
us from freeing ourselves from preconceived opinions.
The authority of Aristotelian metaphysics is perpetuated through a language especially adapted to our
day to day needs-action - and highly misleading in
so far as our intellectual needs are concerned. Only
a language which treats of intellectual matters in
terms of purely intellectual items can familiarise
the scholastically trained philosopher and the layman with the new science. It might be too simple
an explanation to account for Descartes' metaphysical
method of presenting his new physics by his fear of
incurring the wrath of the religious authorities -
as Galileo had done. It might well be the case that,
were it not for the rhetorical power of the traditiona

language of metaphysics, the new *language of ideas*
could not have imposed itself on Descartes' contemporaries and successors. When, for instance, three
generations after Descartes, Hume mentions the
"discovery", he says that "sensible qualities lie
not in the body but merely in the senses" and we
are aware that both the arguments from *physics* and
those from *metaphysics* have disappeared. In a way,
for Hume Descartes' metaphysics had done its job
and was replaced by the "language of ideas". From
now on the language of ideas became the only way of
talking about intellectual matters consistent with
the new physics.

*It is therefore safe to assume that, while on the one hand
the principles of the new science would not have imposed themselves on the philosophical world without being clothed in
metaphysical arguments, on the other hand it is equally safe
to assume that the main function of these metaphysical arguments
was to replace the language of "substantial forms", by the
"language of ideas". This is the reason why Hume with his
"metaphysics of existent ideas" could tell us to commit all
books of divinity or school metaphysics to the flames (E 165).*

If one takes Descartes' achievement to consist in
incorporating the non-animistic approach of Galilean
physics in philosophy -- and in this sense we are
still predominantly Cartesians -- we cannot fail to
be surprised by the fact that the straightforward
scientific approach of the *Regulae* or *Le Monde* could
not have done the job of universalising the new concept of scientific objectivity. Why, for instance,
the following well-known passage from the *Rules for
the Direction of the Mind* was not deemed sufficiently
clear and convincing by Descartes and he shelved
his manuscript and left it unpublished? Here is the
passage concerning the way to deal with a question
such as the nature of the magnet:

"Firstly, in every 'question' there must be something of which we are ignorant; otherwise there
is no use asking the question. Secondly, this
very matter must be designated in some way or
other; otherwise there would be nothing to determine us to investigate it rather than anything

else. Thirdly, it can only be so designated by
the aid of something else which is already known."
(HR I 49)

Even this apparently most innocent first principle
of scientific enquiry entailed a complete reversal
in the procedure of Aristotelian physics. If we
put together Descartes' later remarks concerning
the way we attribute knowledge to the falling stone
with the above injuction to distinguish clearly between the unknown we must posit in every question
we want to solve and what we already know, we can
begin to understand the importance and the difficulty
of uprooting the old habits. The meaning of what
Descartes writes in the *Regulae* about the absolute
necessity of positing an "unknown something" in our
attempt to solve any question lies in its contrast
with the lazy way of substituting for discovery,
inquiry, and method, the transformation of an "unknown something" into a known thing by a linguistic
legerdemain. If for instance we want to know what
is heat, or in Descartes' words, the nature of heat,
and we want to follow Rule XIII of the *Regulae*, we
have to abstain from transforming the quest for knowledge (a quest implying in the strong sense of implying, an unknown explanation which we posit as
our aim) into a verbal exercise which creates a
fiction called "substantial form" or "real quality"
and believe that it exists in the fire and causes
in us the sentiment of heat. By projecting into
the fire the feeling of heat we have practically
cancelled the "unknown" explanation and relieved
ourselves of the tension which could have led us
from the sentiment to the cause of the sentiment.

It is, however, naive to assume that it would have
been enough for Descartes to give his alternative
solution to the question of what is heat in terms
of corporeal motion in order to get rid of substantial forms in scientific explanations:

"Lorsqu'elle brûle [la flamme], ou quelque autre
semblable matière, nous pouvons voir à l'oeil
qu'elle remue les petites parties de ce bois,
et les sépare l'une de l'autre, transformant

ainsi les plus subtiles en feu, en air, et an
fumée, et laissant les plus grossières pour les
cendres. Qu'un autre donc s'imagine, s'il veut,
en ce bois, la forme du feu, la qualité de chaleur,
et l'action qui le brûle, comme des choses toutes
diverses; pour moi qui crains de me tromper si
j'y suppose quelque chose de plus que ce que je
vois nécessairement y devoir être, je me contente
d'y concevoir le mouvement de ses parties."
(Alquié I 319-320)

One could not imagine a more subtle criticism of
scholastic conceptions and a more suggestive presentation of mechanistic philosophy in its application
to the question of the nature of heat. Nevertheless,
even the indirect and ironical refutation of the
substantial forms was considered by Descartes as too
offensive and anyhow ineffective in dislodging the
preconceived opinions. The reason for this ineffec-
tiveness was simply that the world of "real qualities", of heat *in* the fire, was by far more familiar
than the explanation of heat in terms of motion in
the flame.

Besides, the Cartesian explanation was not as simple
as it is presented in the above-quoted passage from
Le Monde. To complete it we have to bring in Descartes' theory of "simple natures". The explanation
of heat by the motion of particles in the fire is
part of a comprehensive reductionism which meant,
in Cartesian philosophy as expressed in the *Regulae*
at least, that all physical phenomena could ultimately be understood in terms of the fundamental
properties of physical particles. Descartes calls
the phenomena to be explained "composite natures"
and the fundamental properties of physical particles
(posited at the outset of any attempt to solve a
question) "simple natures". However, while a commonsensical approach would expect Descartes to say
that his explanation goes from the known to the
unknown, this is exactly what his reductionist
theory in terms of simple and composite natures
leads him to reject. Simple natures will function
upon his theory as independent causes and composite
natures as dependent effects. Ultimately the "un-

known" is explained by the relation of the simple
natures to the known composite natures. Facts may
help to discover a theory but do not explain it, it
is the theory which explains facts. So it could not
be said that there was in Descartes' reductionism
something intrinsically metaphysical which led him
to invert the direction of scientific explanation.

When Descartes introduces the division of things
into natures he emphasises the point that the desig-
nation and the division of things into simple and
composite is made in function of their accessibility
to the understanding:

> "We come secondly to the things themselves which
> must be considered only in so far as they are
> objects of the understanding. From this point
> of view we divide them into the class (1) of those
> whose nature is of the extremest simplicity and
> (2) of the complex and composite." (HR I 27)

The issue of accessibility is crucial and ambiguous.
It is crucial because accessibility to the understanding means and implies that we shall count as
knowledge only that which is not beyond our capacity
to know, i.e. our understanding. Descartes' project
is not, as some have tried to argue, to prove the
possibility of knowledge but rather to circumscribe
the possibilities of our understanding in its quest for
knowledge, a quest Descartes wanted to qualify by
qualifying its limits. Accessibility is ambiguous
because it can be shown to conduce to some form of
idealism and its concomitant inbuilt gap between
our understanding and the external world. So in the
end, those who want to interpret Descartes' project
as an attempt to prove the possibility of knowledge are
obviously starting from the ambiguous meaning of
"accessibility".

As we shall try to show later, all the sceptical and
idealistic interpretations of Cartesianism are the
result of the failure to assess Descartes' intention
in constructing his theory of knowledge in terms of
accessibility to the understanding. Basically speaking, when Locke and Hume will stress the limitation

of our understanding they will be expressing in their
own way Descartes' notion of accessibility to the
understanding. Thus in Rule XII Descartes explains
the composite natures:

"Sixthly, we say that those natures which we call
composite are known by us, either because experience shows us that they are, or because we ourselves are responsible for their composition.
Matter of experience consists of what we perceive
by sense, what we hear from the lips of others,
and generally whatever reaches our understanding
either from external sources or from that contemplation which our mind directs backwards on itself." (HR I 43-44)

This Cartesian concept of experience is, generally
speaking, also the concept of the Empiricists; however, it is not their concept of experience in terms
of ideas or perceptions. In order to understand how,
out of a commonsensical notion of experience which
all Cartesians accepted, the Empiricists evolved
their notion of experience as made of existing entities in the mind, we must follow Descartes in his
translation of his thoughts as expressed in his
earlier logical and scientific writings into the
metaphysical language of his later works.

As we mentioned earlier, reductionism led Descartes
to assert that we deduce the composite natures from
the simple. In fact, the notion of simple natures
is introduced as a postulate:

"Now we must approach the second part of our task.
That was to distinguish accurately the notions of
simple things from those which are built out of
them; to see in both cases where falsity might
come in, so that we might be on our guard and
give our attention to those matters only in which
certainty was possible. But here, as before, we
must make some assumptions which probably are not
agreed by all. It matters little, however, though
they are not believed to be more real than those
imaginary circles by means of which Astronomers
describe their phenomena, provided that you employ
them to aid you in discerning in each particular

case what sort of knowledge is true and what
false." (HR I 40)

It is of the utmost importance to remember this
passage from Rule XII and also what Descartes writes
immediately after. Composite natures when considered
in their real nature are prior to simple natures,
yet when considered from the analytical point of
view, i.e. relatively to our knowledge, they come
after the simple natures which are by definition
unanalysable and hence known by themselves:

> "Thus for example, if we consider a body as having
> extension and figure, we shall admit that from
> the point of view of the thing itself it is one
> and simple. For we cannot from that point of
> view regard it as compounded of corporeal nature,
> extension and figure, since these elements have
> never existed in isolation from each other. But
> relatively to our understanding we call it a
> compound constructed out of these three natures,
> because we have thought of them separately before
> we were able to judge that all three were found
> in one and same subject." (HR I 40)

So when subsequently in the *Meditations* and in the
Principles Descartes will assert that he has demonstrated the deducibility of all our knowledge from
the knowledge of the existence of thought and the
proof of the existence of God, when he reaches the
Meditations we are left with one class of simple
natures, the class of clear and distinct ideas. In
the *Rules for the Direction of the Mind* we are led to
expect that, since simple natures are on principle
unanalysable, there would be three possible appli-
cations of the Rules: the first to spiritual simple
natures, the second to corporeal simple natures,
and the third to simple natures which are at once
spiritual and corporeal. One could formulate our
question as follows: why at the level of the method,
Descartes needs three classes of postulated simple
natures and at the metaphysical level he is content
with one and unique class - the spiritual simple
natures?

In the context of Descartes' *Reply to Objections VI* we
have noticed that in fact he needed two kinds of
rhetorical presentation to convince and persuade
his readers: the metaphysical in terms of Principles
and of deducibility from first causes, and the ideational in terms of sentiments in the mind and their
causes in the object. While the metaphysical way
of presenting his method in physics was the "natural"
manner of advancing an alternative to scholastic
metaphysics, the presentation of his new science in
terms of ideas reflected in a more vivid way the
actual practice of science. The elements of the
analytical reductionist method which he developed
in the *Regulae* were, as we have tried to show, in
a manner, the beginnings of the hypothetico-deductive
methods. The latter Descartes developed by reflecting on the applicability of mathematical and algebraic methods to the relation between theories and
facts. Thus, he will evolve the idea that the solution of all questions in physics could, like in
algebra, be furthered if we divide the question into
known and unknown quantities, represent these quantities by variables and end with equations to be
solved by the algebraic method. By keeping in the
solution the algebraic symbols it would remain quite
clear how the unknown quantity depends on the known:
the principle being to arrive at a clear and distinct
knowledge of all the elements going into the question
before and after its solution. If we add to this
the important suggestion that "imaginary" (in the
sense of not existing as such in real nature) quantities such as simple natures are introduced, we can
understand in what sense the solution of the problem
could be said, according to Descartes, to depend, or
to be the "effect" of these simple natures.

We are now in a position to surmise that the method
pursued by Descartes in the *Meditations* is in a way a
fusion between the metaphysical traditional method
of presenting knowledge (principles as first causes
from which all knowledge is deduced), the analytic-
reductionist method based on the evolvement from
experience of theories which have later to confirm
experience, and last but not least the reduction of
all the classes of simple natures to one class: the

mental. This fusion could help us in elucidating
the different levels at which we can grasp the nature
of distinct and clear ideas. At the level of the
method developed in the *Regulae*, the ideas are known
by themselves, independent, and in so far as the
understanding is aware of them they exist prior to
anything explained in function of them. But in the
Regulae Descartes compared the existent ideas to the
Astronomers' imaginary circles by which they explain
other phenomena. However, if we recall that the
logical simple natures which apply to both corporeal
and spiritual natures are also incorporated in the
spiritual ones in both the *Discourse* and the *Meditations*,
since anyhow we remain with only clear and distinct
ideas, we can understand how the latter came to
include in themselves the logical notion of possible
existence. Ideas include in their meaning the coerciveness of possible existence or the notion of con-
ceivability and that of impossible existence or
inconceivability. So relative to the understanding
ideas are known by themselves and besides they are
logical coerciveness itself. But what about their
actual existence, that which Descartes will call their
objective reality which is dependent on a cause?

The reduction of all simple natures to one class, the
class of mental simple natures, could only succeed
if the notion of simple nature implied the distinction of the mental from the corporeal. This distinction meant that knowledge was the discovery of
an unknown thing and not the discovery of something
"manufactured and composed" by our ideas. In doing
physics, Descartes always assumed that sentiments
and ideas are caused by some unknown cause in the
body, i.e. the working hypothesis tacitly assumed
in physics was the causal theory of perceptions.

So in the end it was the practice of the new science
that led Descartes to incorporate in the notion or
the term "idea" in addition to its explanatory and
logical power its actual existence. Seen in this
light the term "idea" could be well grasped as ful-
filling the multiple tasks it fulfils in the later
philosophy of Descartes: as a metaphysical first
cause or principle, as a logical principle, as a

methodological theoretical entity, and last but not
least as the existing known effect from which we
start to discover the unknown cause. In the long
run the development and dissemination of Cartesianism
will be done mainly through the apparently restricted
notion of the idea as a purely mental existent entity distinct from its material cause. But if our
analysis of the various ingredients amalgamated in
the term "idea" is right, it would not be too difficult to show how all the essentials of the new
scientific method came to be connotated by it. Nor
would it be ununderstandable how the logical and the
metaphysical arguments of the *Meditations* were less
persuading than Descartes' straightforward account
of how he actually evolved the realm of ideas as
distinct from their causes in his reflection on the
new way of doing physics.

If the world of physics was becoming less and less
familiar when mechanical causes came to replace the
cosy world of substantial forms, there was nothing
unfamiliar in the sentiment itself out of which the
substantial fictional form was manufactured. On
the contrary, it retained its familiar character
and extended it to the mind of man. The familiarity
of man with his own soul was certainly not the main
objective of Cartesianism, what Descartes wanted
was to familiarise man with the new "alien world"
of particles in motion through man's familiarity
with his own sentiments. It is true, human sentiments, in the manner Descartes says we are aware of
them, are not exactly the same sentiments we usually
perceive. If in common practice someone says: "I
feel pain in my tooth" part of what he says is true
according to Descartes and part is false. Provided
we take pains to be localised only in the mind - the
state of being aware that one is in pain - then
pains are sentiments in the Cartesian sense. So it
might well be the case that human sentiments broadly
speaking are things with which everyone is familiar
and yet human sentiments in the Cartesian sense are
things which one needs some effort to familiarise
with. Moreover, if we take into account the contemporary attempts to assess, criticise, or even
reject the Cartesian notion of sentiment, then the

only conclusion we must reach is that we are indeed
very far from the Cartesian meaning of the term
"sentiment".

In R.F. Brissenden's article, "'Sentiment': Some
Uses of the Word in the Writings of David Hume",
we are given a survey of a variety of uses of the
term "sentiment" in Hume's philosophy and in the
eighteenth century in general. The range of uses
spans from "sentiment" standing for a theory, an
opinion, a thought, to "sentiment" standing for
feeling, emotion, passion. But also "sentiment"
can stand for simple physical awareness and simple
mental awareness. In Descartes, "sentiment" stands
sometimes for the idea as a purely mental awareness,
whether of a physical or mental cause, sometimes
for the "idea" in the imagination, that is an image
which is rather physical than mental, and sometimes
for a feeling or a passion.[1] But when Descartes,
in the opening paragraph of his physical treatise
Le Monde, speaks of sentiment or the idea we have in
the imagination, he is surely alluding to something
purely mental totally distinct from its corporeal
cause. As we shall show in the next two chapters
on Hume, the terms "idea", "sentiment", "thought",
when taken in the Cartesian sense of mental awareness, carried with this Cartesian sense all the
other uses of the notion of simple natures, uses
which forged and crystallised the new concept of
scientific objectivity.

Thus, Descartes insists that simple natures are in
relation to the understanding, known by themselves,
independent, and cannot contain anything false:

"Thirdly we assert that all these simple natures
are known per se and are wholly free from falsity.
It will be easy to show this, provided we distinguish the faculty of our understanding by which
it has intuitive awareness of things and knows
them, from that by which it judges, making use
of affirmation and denial. For we may imagine
ourselves to be ignorant of things which we really
know, for example on such occasions as when we
believe that in such things over and above what

we have present to us or attain to by thinking,
there is something else hidden from us, and when
this belief of ours is false. Whence it is evident that we are in error if we judge that any
one of these simple natures is not completely
known by us. For if our mind attains to the
least acquaintance with it, as must be the case,
since we are assumed to pass judgment on it, this
fact alone makes us infer that we know it completely. For otherwise it could not be said to
be simple, but must be complex - a compound of
that which is present in our perception of it,
and that of which we think we are ignorant."
(HR I 42)

It is obvious from the above quotation that it is
quite impossible to understand what Descartes will
assert about the indubitability of the Cogito independently of what he writes about the knowledge *per
se* we have of simple natures. In other words, if
we concentrate solely on what Descartes asserts
about the self-evidence of the content of our mental
consciousness and consider this evidence as the first
principle from which he will deduce all the rest of
our knowledge, we shall be overlooking the process
by which Descartes came to replace his theory of
simple natures by *his theory of one simple nature: the
spiritual*.

The typical case Descartes is alluding to in the
above quotation is when one assumes more than one
can perceive clearly and thus attributes sensible
qualities such as colour, taste, and other similar
"real qualities" to objects. But, since this judgment in the light of the *new science of physics is
false*, Descartes infers that he is in error to assume
that there is in the object something hidden over
and above what is present to him. And since, he
adds, we *do* distinguish the true from the false, the
simple natures cannot contain anything false.

The assumption of something existent in objects over
and above what we have present to us or attain by
thinking being false according to modern physics,

one has to conclude that all that is present to the
understanding is clear, not hidden, and *known by
itself*. We have here of course a close connexion
between the notion of a datum of the understanding -
the clear and distinct idea - and the notion of a
theoretical entity which might even have an imaginary existence and still help us to understand
known phenomena. But the difficulty in understanding
the Cartesian notion of evidence is anchored in our
tendency to take what is evident in the solution of
a question as that which is given, the known, in
terms of which the unknown is explained. But, as
we noted before, the Cartesian evidence functions
as the minimum theoretical assumption which explains
the known data.

Ultimately the theory of simple natures, the notion
of evidence, and of clear and distinct ideas are
Descartes' way of expressing his rejection of scholastic metaphysics, for it assumed that there is in
objects something over and above what we can perceive in them, hidden qualities which, when admitted,
the notion of evidence becomes vacuous. If whatever
we do we have never enough material to decide about
a question, then it becomes clear that there are no
criteria for deciding either way in the solution of
any question. Obviously, Descartes thought that
scholastically trained thinkers did decide and
delude themselves that they solved the question they
wanted to solve, and their delusion was that they
understood the object in terms of their sentiments.
Such scholastic solutions were false according to
Descartes and besides they were ultimately verbal
solutions and not discoveries of truth.

Solutions of problems can be made solely in terms
of what is knowable in principle, and when the knowable in principle is contrasted with the hidden or
what is over and above what is present to us, it
becomes the evidence of which we have an intuitive
awareness, the simple natures which are *wholly free
from falsity: known per se*. On the other hand, Descartes
constantly reminds us in the *Regulae* that the simple
natures in terms of which we explain objects do not
ever exist in isolation and compared to objects (the

composite natures) the simple natures are more real
only in relation to the understanding.

So it appears that those commentators who have tried
to understand Cartesian philosophy as founded on
incorrigible, self-verifying, indubitable propositions about the facts of consciousness or states of
mind have totally overlooked the transformation of
Descartes' philosophy of science into the mataphysics
of the *Meditations*. Descartes was always concerned
with the difficulties he was facing in trying to
formulate his conception of scientific objectivity
in a manner which would convince and persuade the
scholastically trained reader. It might well have
been the case that he slowly arrived at the conclusion that the problem of explaining his physics
was to be conceived as yet another "question to be
solved", a question analogous to such questions he
mentions in the *Regulae* as "what is the nature of
the magnet" or "what is the nature of sound" (HR I 49).

On this hypothesis, the *Meditations* become an extension
of Descartes' *Regulae* by making "the nature of the
understanding" like any other question. We must
firstly assume something of which we are ignorant,
secondly the matter of the question must be designated some way or other and thirdly it must be
designated by the aid of something which is already
known (see HR I 49). This extension of the Cartesian
scientific method to the discovery of the nature of
the understanding gives us a theory of mind by which
we can explain all data about the mind - data made
of composite natures of course. But it was also
meant to dislodge the pseudo-notions of evidence
used in scholastic metaphysics and to replace them
by the Cartesian conception of evidence indispensable for the discovery of the true nature of the
understanding.

In the *Regulae* Descartes is already persuaded and
convinced that the intellectual simple natures are
known independently of any corporeal image:

"Those are purely intellectual which our understanding apprehends by means of a certain inborn

light, and without the aid of any corporeal image.
That a number of such things exist is certain; and it is
impossible to construct any corporeal idea which
shall represent to us what the act of knowing is,
what doubt it, what ignorance, and likewise what
the action of the will is which it is possible
to term volition, and so with other things."
(HR I 41)

In a word, the distinction between mind and body
which will become the supreme aim of the *Meditations*
is assumed as obvious and in no need of demonstration,
and there is no hint that the distinction would become the ultimate principle of Cartesian metaphysics.
Descartes does not seem even to conceive that those
intellectual things, the intellectual simple natures
such as doubt or ignorance, are in need of any further characterisation:

"Yet we have a genuine knowledge of all these
things, and know them so easily that in order
to recognise them it is enough to be endowed with
reason." (HR I 41)

But the more he tried to communicate his new conception of knowledge, the more he found that the cardinal difference between his new conception and that
of the Scholastics depended on his new notion of
what is an evidence. Further, the more he reflected
on his notion of evidence, the more he discovered
that it depended on his notion of the understanding.
Again his notion of the understanding rested on two
assumptions: a) that knowledge is accessible to the
understanding and b) that what is not accessible
is not knowledge. *The inaccessability to the understanding*
of all the scholastic "species", "real qualities",
"substantial forms" led Descartes to the conclusion
that all our belief in the existence of these entities is false. The inability of the understanding
to conceive all these occult scholastic entities
meant that the understanding could only conceive
simple natures which contain nothing which is inacc-
essible.

In the *Meditations* Descartes therefore tries to solve

the question of "what is the nature of the understanding", the seat of all our inutitive knowledge
of things known *per se* : the criterion of whatever is
accessible to us as knowledge. Could we have a
knowledge of the understanding itself without believing that there is in the nature of the understanding something "over and above" what we have
present to us? Could we have an awareness of what
is the understanding without assuming something
hidden of which we are desperately ignorant? An
easy answer to these questions would be that the
criterion by which we know simple natures *per se*
must also itself be known similarly. Could such
an answer based on logic, i.e. on common notions
which are ascribed equally to spiritual and to corporeal things, give us the nature of the understanding? But already in the *Regulae,* Descartes has
declared that

> "these common notions can be discerned by the
> understanding either unaided or when it is aware
> of the images of material things." (HR I 42)

The question "what is the nature of the understanding" will have to be answered without assuming anything over and above the understanding, without
assuming anything hidden, without assuming any
logical principle: the understanding must be discovered when we are in doubt about all what the
understanding can achieve as knowledge. In a word
we must, if we want to follow the method of the
Regulae, become aware of our understanding prior to
our knowledge of our body, prior to our knowledge
of common notions. The question "what is the nature
of the understanding" is further specified by asking
the question "what is the nature of doubt". In
La Recherche de la Vérité, Eudoxe the Cartesian asks
Poliandre what he is, he who can doubt everything
and who cannot doubt himself. It is only when
Poliandre makes the error to go beyond the limits
of the question put by Descartes that he can with
the help of this error attain the knowledge of what
he is. The previous answer of Poliandre to the
question "what is he, he who doubts everything?"
consisted in obscure metaphysical concepts such as
"corporeal substance", "body", "animated". In his

words:

"Il ya plus, quand pour satisfaire à cette question, j'ai répondu que j'étais un homme, je ne
pensais pas à tous ces êtres scolastiques qui
m'étaient inconnus, et dont je n'avais jamais rien
entendu dire, et qui je pense, n'existent que dans
l'imagination de ceux qui les ont inventés, mais
je voulais parler des choses que nous voyons, que
nous touchons, que nous sentons et que nous
eprouvons en nous-mêmes; en un mot, des choses
que le plus simple des hommes sait aussi bien que
le plus grand philosophe de l'univers; je voulais
dire que je suis un certain tout compose de deux
bras, de deux jambes, d'une tête et de toutes les
autres parties qui constituent ce qu'on appelle
le corps humain, lequel tout, en outre se nourrit,
marche, sent et pense." (Alquié II 1126-27)

At this stage Poliandre has only relinquished the
use of scholastic metaphysical complications and so
he is reminded by Eudoxe of the fact that he is still
going beyond the limit of the question and that he
does not fully understand the question. Subsequently
Poliandre sees his error and declares:

"Et cependant nous avons quelque sujet d'appeler
heureuse l'erreur que j'ai commise, puisque je
lui dois de savoir maintenant que ce que je suis
en tant que je doute, n'est nullement ce que
j'appelle mon corps." (Alquié II 1127)

And Eudoxe will confirm again Poliandre's conclusion:

"Car, comme vous l'avez dit avec raison, c'est
une heureuse erreur que celle que vous avez
commise en dépassant dans votre reponse les
limites de ma question; avec son secours, en
effet, vous pouvez parvenir à la connaissance
de ce que vous êtes, en écartant de vous et en
rejetant tout ce que vous voyez clairement ne
pas vous appartenir, et en n'admettant rien qui
ne vous appartienne si nécessairement que vous
en soyez aussi certain que de votre existence et
de votre doute." (Alquié II 1131)

The purpose of bringing at this stage this long
quotation from *La Recherche de la Vérité* is to show
that the solution of the question "what is the
understanding" follows the same pattern of reasoning
Descartes makes in the *Regulae* when he proves the
doctrine of the simple natures known *per se*. In both
cases it is shown that the error which is due to
the thrust of reason going beyond the limit of the
understanding is a beneficial error which shows us
how we can avoid it. If in the case of corporeal
simple natures they are proved to be known *per se*
after avoiding the error of attributing to objects
colours and other similar qualities, in the case
of the understanding itself it is demonstrated to
be known *per se* after avoiding the error of attributing to it (that is to the doubting person) a
corporeal existence.

We are still very far from the notion of what we
call nowadays the introspective certainty of the
Cogito. The Occam razor principle Descartes applies
in order to evolve the notion of the understanding
limiting itself to the strictly necessary kind of
theoretical entities - necessary to explain the
world of experience - is generalised from the practice of physics to the practice of all intellectual
activities. What we need to understand of all physical
phenomena are the simple natures such as figure,
extension, motion, etc. and what we need to understand of mental phenomena is thought; and both,
i.e. extension and thought, are in relation to the
understanding prior to the phenomena they explain
and hence known *per se*. But when Descartes is urged
by the still unconvinced and unpersuaded Aristotelian
who is represented by Epistemon to clarify what is
thinking, what is doubting, he can no longer answer
that these things which are used to explain other
complex things cannot be explained in their turn.

The question Epistemon is asking is an indication
that the formal demonstration has failed to reach
its proposed effect. Perhaps the failure of this
metaphysical proof to convince Epistemon is due to
the fact that he is not versed in the new science
or because he continues to ask questions in the

tradition of scholastic disputations expecting definitions in terms of "the nearest genus" and the
"essential difference". Doubt, thought, and existence are among those things which are so clear
that they are known by themselves, answers Eudoxe,
and he insists that

> "J'ajoute qu'il est impossible d'apprendre ces
> choses autrement que de soi-même, et d'en être
> persuadé autrement que par sa propre expérience,
> et par cette conscience ou ce témoignage intérieur
> que chaque homme trouve en lui-même quand il
> examine une observation quelconque; de telle
> sorte que, comme il serait inutile de définir ce
> que c'est le blanc pour le faire comprendre à
> un aveugle, tandis que pour le connaître il nous
> suffit d'ouvrir les yeux et de voir du blanc, de
> même, pour savoir ce que c'est que le doute et
> la pensée, il suffit de douter et de penser."
> (Alguié II 1136-1137)

The passage from things "known by themselves" to
things "which cannot be learnt except from ourselves"
is the passage Descartes felt he must make in order
to familiarise his readers with the theoretical entities known *per se*. The passage consists in endow-
ing the theoretical entities posited by the new
science whether in the physical world or in the
mind with the characteristics of men's personal
experience and their sentiments.

Being prior to objects in relation to the understanding is obviously a common characteristic to
both the corporeal and the spiritual simple natures.
The "objects" in the realm of the corporeal are
that with which everybody is familiar. Similarly
the "objects" to be explained in the realm of the
intellectual are familiar to everybody since every
man thinks and doubts. The simple corporeal natures
are the *understandable* theoretical assumed entities
which can be thought separately though they have
never existed in isolation from each other. There
would be no possibility, according to Descartes, to
distinguish the false from the true were it not for
the fact that simple corporeal natures are known *per se*.

The paradigm error is that of the scholastics who projected our sentiments into the objects. The whole of the new science is equated by Descartes to the replacement of "hidden qualities" by the simple natures known by themselves. In trying to resolve the question "what is the nature of the understanding" Descartes uses "the happy error" which consists in answering any question by giving "over and above" what is strictly necessary to explain the nature of mind. "The happy error" in the case of the physical world is the transference of thought to the falling stone, in the case of doubt is thinking that we cannot explain what we are when we are doubting without bringing in our corporeal existence. However, it is one thing to say that everyone is familiar with what it is to think and to doubt, it is another thing to say that everyone is familiar with that which is strictly necessary to explain without error the nature of doubt. The world of physical objects is a familiar world: the realm of figure, motion, extension, of corporeal simple natures is an understandable realm which explains the world of familiar objects. When we come to the explanation of our intellectual powers that which is familiar fuses with that which is understandable: the "introspective certainty of our doubt" fuses with Descartes' certainty that doubt is non-corporeal. But while the latter is theoretically *the known per se,* the former is directly known: we need no intermediary steps to be acquainted with it: "il suffit d'ouvir les yeux et de voir du blanc" in order to know what it is to be "blanc".

Thus the distinction between mind and body which is essential to the practice of the new physics is also essential to the understanding of the nature of mind; and the knowledge of the nature of mind becomes the knowledge which is prior, in relation to the under- standing, to the knowledge of the material world. In the *Meditations* Descartes effectuates a further reduction and his metaphysics will make knowledge in general deducible from the most general principles which are clear and evident:

"I have taken the being or existence of this thought as the first principle... (HR I 208)

says Descartes referring (in the "Author's Letter
to the Translator" of *The Principles of Philosophy*) to
the fact that he who doubts all things cannot doubt
that he exists while he doubts. The first principle
from which Descartes deduces all knowledge including
the knowledge of God's existence is the "thought
that he who doubts must exist". Such a thought is
obviously of the same nature as our thought: "that
which falls must have figure and extension" and
nothing more. The *Cogito* is the first principle
because it is a *simple nature known per se* and our
knowledge of other simple natures depends on it.
The certainty of our experiences, our thoughts,
doubts, feelings, in short our introspective certainty is not the foundation of the indubitability
of the *Cogito*. On the contrary, it is the latter
which endows the former with a new meaning. Through
the *Cogito* we are not only aware of the existence of
our sentiments but we are also aware that these
sentiments are not physical objects. Philosophy did not
wait for Descartes in order to discover that men
are familiar with and certain of the existence of
their sentiments. Nor did Descartes' first principles consist in this current certainty of one's
feelings. But what is true is that Descartes did
use the notion of the certainty of one's experiences
in order to popularise the notion that experiences,
thoughts, sentiments are not similar to the things
which cause them.

It must have occurred to Descartes that in order to
eradicate once and for all the vestiges of the scholastic explanation of the relation between the operations of the senses and the intellect, the best
way would be to start with human sentiments with
which every man is familiar. In this context one
can understand the crucial importance of the sentiments which heat can cause in men. Since the same
heat can sometimes cause pain and sometimes pleasure
and since it is comparatively easy to show that pain
cannot exist in the fire, it is understandable why
the example of the sensation of heat is the standard
example used by all Cartesians; Locke,
Arnauld and Nicole, Malebranche, Berkeley, and Hume,
in order to illustrate the importance of the doctrine

of ideas and how the doctrine came to replace the
theory of substantial forms. In Rule XII of the
Regulae Descartes is well aware that he is advancing
one "doctrine" in place of another.

"Secondly we must believe that while the external
sense is stimulated by the object, the figure
which is conveyed to it is carried off to some
other part of the body, that part called the
common sense, in the very same instant and without the passage of any real entity from one to
the other." (HR II 37-38)

The French translation conveys even more strongly
Descartes' intention to get rid of the "doctrine"
of substantial forms which rested on the supposition
that some sort of "beings" were transferred in sense
perception. Instead of "without the passage of any
real entity from one place to the other" we have:

"sans qu'il y ait passage réel d'aucun être d'un
endroit à l'autre."

If the Cogito did only establish the distinction
between mind and body by the possibility of knowing
the first independently of the second it would be
easy to consider the Cogito as the first principle
of physics. The latter depended solely on the rejection of "real entities" passing from the object
to the mind. Once the sentiment is taken as essentially dissimilar to its cause in the object, the
way is open for the rejection of all the obsure
"entities" assumed in the scholastic theory of knowledge and their replacement by clear and distinct
ideas in the mind. But the Cogito, as a first principle, naturally assumed a further metaphysical
dimension: the other two principles, the proof of
the existence of God and of the material world were
deducible from it. The Cogito, in a metaphysical
system, naturally assumed the function of the ultimate Simple Nature known *per se* and which explains
the other principles. Moreover, the Cogito, as we
saw from *La Recherche de la Vérité*, is equated with oux
familiar awareness of our own sentiments, and the
introspective certainty is by this equation trans-

formed into the indubitability of things known *per
se* - in relation to the understanding. What is posited as simple, known by itself, in the realm of
theory construction to explain the usually known
facts, that which exists prior to facts in relation
to the understanding - in short the minimum speculative principle needed for the construction of
the true science, the Cogito becomes the familiar
awareness of every person of his own perceptions,
sentiments, thoughts. If we sever our usual awareness of our thoughts, our introspective certainty,
from the speculative theoretical function of the
Cogito in relation to physics, the importance of
the doctrine of ideas as the "discovery" which is
responsible for the considerable advances in physics
is totally ununderstandable.

We have to distinguish two consequences of the fusion in the Cogito of the speculative principle of
the successful new science on the one hand, and of
the direct acquaintance each person has with his
own thoughts on the other. The first consequence
is that we stop believing in an anthropomorphic
world fabricated on the model of our soul. All the
domain of our introspective awareness had to be
identified with the purely mental, the non-corporeal,
otherwise all our prejudices of childhood will remain with us. That is why Descartes, in his *Principles of Philosophy* at the end of Part I and before
repeating the errors we must avoid in order to phil-
osophise correctly, returns to the paradigmatic
case of introspective certainty each person experiences when feeling pain - (obviously because it
is the strongest certainty one could feel and because it is equally obvious that pain does not exist
outside our mind.) Descartes wants to include in
our introspective certainty about our sensations
something which would prevent us from making wrong
judgments with these sensations:

> *"That we frequently deceive ourselves in judging of pain
> itself.*

The same is true in regard to all our other sensations, even those which have to do with agreeable sensation and pain. For although we do not

believe that these feelings exist outside of us,
we are not wont to regard them as existing merely
in the mind or our perception, as being in our
hands, feet, or some other part of our body.
But there is no reason that we should be obliged
to believe that the pain, for example, which we
feel in our foot, is anything beyond our mind
which exists in our foot, nor that the light
which we imagine ourselves to see in the sun
really is in the sun (as it is in us); for both
these are prejudices of our youth, as will
clearly appear in what follows." (HR I 247)

Descartes' suggestion is that introspective certainty left to itself without bad habits due to wrong
judgments would reveal to us the purely *mental nature*
of all our feelings, sensations, and ideas. It is
of course doubtful whether without the impact of
the new science men could reach this vision of the
pure non-corporeal nature of our sensations.

The second consequence of the fusion in the Cogito
of the principle of the new science and of the capacity we have to be aware directly of our own sensations was that sentiments were transformed into
the first principles of science. *The world of matter
may have become utterly unfamiliar but the principles from
which men could deduce all their knowledge of the world of
matter were simple, clear, distinct, introspectively known.
By changing the meaning of our introspective certainty,
Descartes has been able to convey in a new language, the
language of ideas, his most speculative doctrine about the
nature of the world of matter.*

Basically, Descartes' works are all about the same
subject: the need for a conceptual linguistic reform in order to be able to communicate the revolutionary findings of the new science. Starting with
the *Regulae* he enunciates the principles of the new
physics in terms of a radical change in method. He
is not yet aware of the great difficulties in changing the intellectual habits which prevent his readers
from accepting what is for him already clear and
evident. When he was writing his books on physics

he took for granted that mental and corporeal things
are entirely distinct and that what was false in the
old science was due to the blurring of the distinction between mind and body. Gradually he grasped
that the animistic and the anthropomorphic errors
of scholastic science could be more easily avoided
if he freed the mind of any corporeal entity than
by trying to present matter as entirely devoid of
any human sentiment.

At this stage he was ready to present his science
in a metaphysical language starting from principles
known *per se*, i.e. from some thing existing prior
to anything else, that is at the speculative theoretical level. From the thought that he who doubts
must exist he deduces that there is a God who is
the author of all that is in the world and who does
not deceive us when we judge on the basis of clear
and distinct perceptions. The two principles, the
Cogito and the existence of a non-deceiver God, are
all Descartes needs for explaining all immaterial
or metaphysical things. The third principle which
is deduced from the first two is that there are
bodies which are extended in length, breadth and
depth, which have diverse figures and move in diverse
ways:

> "These, in sum are all the principles from which
> I deduce the truth of other things." (HR I 209)

All this highly abstract metaphysical presentation
of the method of the new science could perhaps convince but not yet persuade the readers of Descartes'
writings. To be persuaded even Descartes himself
needed the actual explanations of physics in terms
of the new language of ideas. Provided we do not
overlook the two ingredients in the meaning of the
term "idea", a) its meaning as a simple nature
which in relation to the understanding, i.e. at the
theoretical and speculative level, exists prior to
anything which is explained in terms of it; b) its
meaning as an item of introspective awareness indubitable and purely mental - we can now understand
how in the *Reply to Objections VI* the language of ideas
describing the practice of physics is the language

which will persuade both Descartes and his readers.
Here again is the crucial passage:

"But after I had noted these things with sufficient care, and had accurately distinguished
the idea of mind from the ideas of body and corporeal movement, and had discovered that all my
previous ideas of real qualities or substantial
forms had been composed or manufactured by me
out of the former set of ideas, I easily released
myself from all the doubts that are here advanced.
For firstly I had no doubt that I possessed a
clear idea of my own mind, of which naturally I
had the most intimate knowledge, nor could I
doubt that that idea was wholly diverse from the
idea of other things, and contained within it no
element of corporeity. For since I had thought
to find out the true ideas of all other things
as well and seemed to have a general acquaintance
with all of them, I found nothing in them which
was not wholly different from the idea of the
mind." (HR II 255)

In contrast with the metaphysical and logical arguments of the *Meditations* where "the idea of mind" is
a first principle from which we deduce "the existence of the mind", the existence of God, and of the
material world, we have in the above passage a
"clear idea of my own mind" of which naturally
Descartes had the most "intimate knowledge", an
idea which is introspectively certain and which is
distinguished from all other ideas of corporeal
things. Our knowledge of both our intellectual
power and of material objects is expressible in
terms of ideas: the distinction itself between mind
and body is expressible in terms of the distinction
between the idea of mind and the idea of body. We
can understand how Descartes by his new usage of
the term, i.e. *by his rhetorical innovation*, could effectuate the conceptual revolution in order to familiarise his readers with the new science.

The Cogito as such could not be used as a Rule for
analysing our knowledge of things: it was a first

Principle of the new speculative science. The
Cogito, however, when taken to be also the indubitable introspective certainty each man has of his
own sentiments led Descartes to formulate what he
calls himself the Rule and which Thomas Reid calls
the Doctrine of Ideas. In a Letter to Père Gibieuf
dated 19 Janvier 1642 Descartes wrote:

> "Mais il en faut revenir a la règle ci-devant
> posée, à savoir, que nous ne pouvons avoir aucune
> connaissance des choses, que par les idées que
> nous en concevons; et que, par conséquent, nous
> n'en devons juger que suivant ces idées, et même
> nous devons penser que tout ce qui répugne à ces
> idées est absolument impossible, et implique
> contradiction." (Alguié II, 907)

And of course the Rule has been already applied
before it is formulated: in the *Reply to Objections VI*
Descartes persuades himself after reformulating his
criticism of the scholastic philosophy in terms of
"ideas". At the level of the language of "ideas"
the absurd confusion of our idea of the mind with
our idea of the body explains Descartes' previous
opinions about real qualities or substantial forms.
If "substantial forms", "occult and real qualities"
are to be eliminated from our language, it is not
enough to deride these entities - as Descartes had
done in *Le Monde*. One must use *a new language* which
exposes the absurdities of the old. The conceptual
reform towards which Descartes was slowly progressing
from the *Regulae* to the *Meditations*, a reform which
was needed to put an end to the authority of the
old philosophy, a reform which would allow us to
treat of intellectual matters in terms of purely
intellectual items, is at last possible when
Knowledge is expressed in terms of Ideas.

When by the end of the next century, Thomas Reid
criticised all Cartesian theories of ideas as con-
tradicting commonsense, he overlooked two important
things. First, that in so far as the relation
language - thought is concerned, he was himself a
Cartesian since he held the view that words are
empty sounds unless they signify our thoughts.

Secondly, in his criticism of the view that knowledge or perception of objects must be justified in
terms of knowledge and perception of ideas, he overlooked the connection between Descartes' Rule and
Descartes' system of metaphysics. He praises the
simplicity of Descartes' metaphysics:

"Of all the systems we know, that of Descartes
was the most remarkable for its simplicity.
Upon one proposition, *I think*, he builds the whole
fabric of human knowledge. And from mere matter,
with a certain quantity of motion given it at
first, he accounts for all the phenomena of the
material world.

The physical part of this system was a mere
hypothesis. It had nothing to recommend it but
its simplicity: yet it had force enough to over-
turn the system of Aristotle, after that system
had prevailed for more than a thousand years."[2]

And, in spite of this praise for Descartes' simple
hypothesis, Reid could never see in the language of
ideas the conceptual reform necessary for the rejection of Aristotelian physics. As a matter of
fact Reid's *Essays on the Intellectual Powers of Man* could
not have been written had the Cartesians not separated the intellectual realm from the corporeal not
only in science but in all intellectual inquiries.

But Reid did not only criticise the Cartesian theory
of knowledge i.e. that our knowledge of things is
always through the mediation of our knowledge of
ideas, he also criticised, and very strongly, the
Cartesian belief in the existence of ideas. There
is no doubt a great difference between assuming the
existence of an entity for the sake of explaining
some phenomenon and concluding that the existence
of the theoretical entity is even more known than
the existence of the things to be explained. When
Descartes introduced the notion of simple natures
in the *Regulae* he compared their status to that of
the imaginary circles which astronomers assume in
order to explain the movements of the stars. But
when he deals with those things which are simple
relatively to our understanding and which are purely

intellectual, Descartes asserts that they are appre-
hended by means of an inborn light and he adds:

> "That a number of such things exist is certain;
> and it is impossible to construct any corporeal
> idea which shall represent to us what the act of
> knowing is, what doubt is, what ignorance ..."
> (HR I 41)

Thus the existence of ideas in the sense of intellectual simple natures is assumed in the *Regulae*, even
though such an existence of a simple nature is never
conceived in isolation of others of the same kind.
The notion of an existent idea is furthered in the
Meditations when Descartes develops his causal theory
of perception and of knowledge, a theory which he
also held when in *Le Monde* he wrote about the sentiment of heat which is *produced* by something in the
flame. However, the existence of ideas becomes
indubitable both on account of the Cogito which
asserts that I who doubt must necessarily, as a mind,
exist, and on account of assimilating our introspective awareness to an awareness of the existence
of thought. The notions of the existence of ideas
is summed up in the following passage of the *Passions
of the Soul* Part First, Article XXV and XXVI. In
Article XXV Descartes reduces all our perceptions
to passions in relation to our soul:

> "But, although all our perceptions, both those
> which we relate to objects which are outside us,
> and those which we relate to the diverse affec-
> tions of our body, are truly passions in respect
> of our soul ..."

And in Article XXVI he expresses the indubitability,
the necessary existence when we are aware of them,
of all our passions:

> "but that we cannot be so deceived regarding the
> passions, inasmuch as they are so close to, and
> so entirely within our soul, that it is impossible
> for it to feel them without their being actually
> such as it feels them to be." (HR I 343)

It appears then, upon our interpretation, that the

age-long debate concerning the logical status of
the Cogito could be closed. In principle one could
not ask the question whether the Cogito is a
syllogism or any other form of argument. It is to
fall into the trap laid by the Tortoise to Achilles
to ask by what logical principle another principle
of logic could be validated. The Cogito is itself
a principle of logic and besides it is a principle
of logic which, when expressed, asserts the necessary existence of the mind, of thought, of ideas.
The notion of the logical nature of ideas is the
consequence of the Rule according to which we cannot have any knowledge of things except by the ideas
which we have of these things: we cannot judge these
things except according to ideas and whatever is
rejected by these ideas is impossible and implies
a contradiction. (See letter to Gibieuf). In a
word, the language of ideas absorbs Logic which is
thus separated from language. Knowledge is not only
defined in purely intellectual mental terms, it is
specifically characterised as non-verbal by nature.

Descartes was obviously one of the main architects
of the view that in so far as our intellectual capacity is concerned, language has no active part to
play. What is not obvious and even doubtful is
whether Descartes has named mental processes and
states, calling them "ideas", and left the nature
of these ideas undecided and by so doing has made
a "conjuring trick" as Wittgenstein wrote in the
Philosophical Investigations. The language of ideas was
not conceived as a language which deals with a specific subject matter: ideas. It was a rhetorical
invention, a new usage of the term "idea" which
could effectively put an end to all notions of knowledge assuming an identity of the entities inside
and outside our minds or of knowledge consisting in
the passage of "beings" from the object to the mind.

To use the language of ideas was, for Descartes, to
subscribe to the Rule or doctrine of ideas. This
doctrine does not make knowledge possible but rather
the possibility of knowledge requires such a rule,
otherwise we would not be able to distinguish the
true from the false. The rule embodies the basic

truth of the distinction between mind and body in
the form of the distinction between the idea of
mind and the ideas of body. The language of ideas
expresses the basic principle of physics, the paradigm of knowledge, the distinction between body
and mind. If the language of ideas alludes to any
state of mind, then it alludes to a state of mind
taking knowledge as an on-going process. Talking
of knowledge in terms of ideas does not mean that
an idea of something constitutes the knowledge of
that thing. On the contrary, it means that knowledge consists always in the answer to a clearly
formulated question. It is not the case that knowledge is by essence problematic from the moment we
sever the evidence in the mind from the object of
knowledge outside the mind. What is called by
modern empiricists the gap between ideas and things
was not meant by Descartes and his followers to be
the "characteristic obsession" of philosophy with
the question: are there, corresponding to ideas,
real qualities in the external world which we can
know through the mediation of ideas? The doctrine
of ideas, the rule without which there would be no
truth or falsehood, defines the problem of knowledge
in the sense that when we proceed to know something
we must be aware of the problem to be solved, define
it in an understandable language, and admit in the
solution to the problem only what is knowable in
principle.

As we have emphasised before, the basic premiss of
Descartes is that we know something, that knowledge
is possible. The break with scholasticism starts
with this assumption and hence with the rule that
in formulating our questions we cannot assume that
there is in objects something over and above what
we can clearly understand. The doctrine of ideas
sums up Descartes' basic rule that theoretical entities needed in explaining any known phenomenon
cannot be obscure, hidden, occult, unknown. And
when the phenomenon to be explained is knowledge,
understanding, then of course we can say that we
are before a problem to be solved, like when we ask
"what is the nature of the magnet?". So when we
know, or doubt, or ignore, what we specifically

must not assume is to suppose something mysterious
or insoluble or unknown to explain the familiar
experience of knowledge, doubt, or ignorance.

There is, indeed there must be, something unknown
at the start of any question otherwise knowledge
would not be an on-going process; but this unknown
is neither the phenomenon to be explained, which
is posited by Descartes as the known, nor the elements out of which the known will be explained, for
these by definition must be better known than the
phenomenon itself, they must be known *per se*. The
unknown is simply the sort of combination of the
simple elements, which would explain the phenomenon.
For example in the case of doubt, an existing thinking mind explains the nature of doubt. It is important to emphasise the difference between the
function of the language of ideas in familiarising
the readers with the speculative foundations of the
new physics and its function in describing human
behaviour.

It might well be the case that what Wittgenstein
criticises in the Cartesian theory of mind is mainly
the result of three centuries of introspective
psychology. But during these centuries the Cartesian
notion of the idea as the criterion for what is
understandable and required in a theory of science,
has probably been lost. Science and its philosophy
have gone one way and introspective psychology has
gone another. And so the neo-Cartesianism of Russell
and Wittgenstein is really an anachronism, and
appeared in the absurd form of anchoring scientific
certainty in some form of introspected sense-data.
The project of Descartes of founding his physics on
the distinction between mind and body and ultimately
on ideas was a project which was justified by the
resistance, his and others', to the new approach to
the world of objects. Descartes' metaphysics is
justified in the sense that it has contributed to
the conceptual reform needed for familiarising the
readers with the new science. What is nowadays
called the search for foundations is often not mot-
ivated by any resistance to science. Science is
universally accepted and might well do without

foundations. In Russell's case it is very likely
that his "Cartesianism" was prompted by wanting to
do for science what he had done for mathematics.
But then this is altogether a project which has
nothing to do with the original Cartesian project.
The language of ideas is used by Descartes to en-
sure that objects are not understood or explained
in terms of human sentiments, it is a language
which ultimately functions as a systematic brack-
eting of human sentiments and thus ensures that
scientific explanations will not contain these
sentiments. When the modern Cartesians use the
language of ideas (or anything standing for ideas)
they reintroduce some subjective elements in scientific explanations.

Notes

1. *Studies in the Eighteenth Century*, ed. R.F. Brissenden,
   Australian National University Press, Canberra,
   1968, pp. 89-107.

2. Thomas Reid, *Essays on the Intellectual Powers of Man*,
   M.I.T.Press, Cambridge, Massachusetts and London,
   1969, pp. 698-699.

CHAPTER V
The Cartesian Hume

The development of the theory of ideas, when applied
to psychology, transformed the theory from a doctrine embodying the speculative principles of physics
into a dubious attempt to ground our knowledge of
the external world in pure subjectivity. Descartes,
were he not intent to eradicate his preconceived
opinions (his adhesion to scholastic ways of thinking),
in order to convince and persuade his readers, might
well have not changed his basic philosophy of science
from its logical and methodical formulation in the
Regulae into its metaphysical and ideational presentation in the *Meditations* and the *Principles*. The traditional, rhetoric, of presenting physics as grounded
in metaphysics besides translating the new principles of science into metaphysical principles, was
also the occasion for Descartes to effectuate a
further step in his reductionist programme.
Descartes' intention was never to replace the corporeal simple natures, figure, extension and motion
in physical explanations by spiritual simple natures,
thought and idea. Nevertheless in the *Meditations*,
the hierarchy of principles is never blurred; the
first principle is the Cogito which with the proof
of the existence of a non-deceiver God allows him
to deduce the third principle asserting that there
are bodies extended in length, breadth and depth,
which have diverse figures and move in diverse ways.

The metaphysical subordination of the corporeal
simple natures to the Cogito was even more pro-
nounced when Descartes fused together the evidential
character of simple natures with the evidential
nature of our introspective awareness. As we have
already stressed in the preceding chapter, this
fusion had two effects first, our sentiments, passions, feelings, thoughts, ideas, volitions, were
all purified from any corporeal ingredient and as
a result we were precluded from projecting them into

the world of objects. Second, these human sentiments thus purified of any corporeal element, were
taken as embodying the first principle of physics: the
distinction between mind and body. These two results were succintly formulated by Descartes in his
Rule which says that we cannot have any knowledge
of things except by the ideas through which we
conceive them. Instead of saying that in relation
to the understanding, extension is known *per se*, is
a corporeal simple nature absolutely distinct from
a spiritual nature like thought or doubt, the
Cartesian Rule allows us to say that our idea of
extension is simple and totally distinct from our
idea of mind. Since anyhow it is at the level of
the understanding that we can determine what is
acceptable and what is not in our practice of science,
so we might as well conduct all our distinctions
in terms of spiritual simple natures: ideas, which
explain the nature of the understanding itself.
This is in effect the persuasive language to which
Descartes resorts in his Reply to the Sixth Objections. The rhetorical innovation of Descartes could
be summed up in his transformation of man's familiarity with his sentiments into man's familiarity
with his ideas felt and conceived as distinct from
external corporeal objects. It is thus quite clear
that the language of ideas far from being the language of subjectivity was introduced and disseminated
as the language of objectivity.

This language of objectivity, the doctrine of ideas,
when applied to physics meant simply that the sentiments or ideas caused by external objects are
dissimilar to that which causes the sentiments, or
as Hume formulates the doctrine: qualities are not
in the objects they are perceptions in the mind. As
such the doctrine seems to be - for us at least -
quite innocuous but in reality it was a simple formulation of a highly complex revolution in man's
relation to nature. For instance, it includes an
injunction not to look for something secret or occult
existing in the object, something which we cannot
understand. Nor should we simply transfer our sentiment into the object and explain a human sentiment
by a similar sentiment in the object. Last but not

least, provided we are aware that our sentiment is
a purely mental entity and distinct from the object
which produces it, we can have or form an idea of
what the object is. Hume's *Treatise* appeared in print
a hundred years after the *Discourse* and the *Meditations*.
Meanwhile Newton had published his *Principia* and his
Optics, and few British thinkers in the first half
of the 18th century would have thought that the new
scientific approach to the study of nature was in
any need of defence: science was more or less a
going concern. So the object of the *Treatise* is to
transfer the scientific method from astronomy and
physics to what Hume calls the moral sciences:
morals, logic and criticism. During these hundred
years the language of ideas was first adopted by
Locke and developed by Berkeley in England, while in
France the Cartesians, Arnauld and Malebranche,
also defended the new scientific objectivity through
their version of the doctrine. In the eyes of Hume,
not only Moral Philosophy would profit from the
application to it of the speculative principles of
physics but also physics itself. In a sense,
Hume was to become more Cartesian than Descartes:
even if he rejected many aspects of Descartes'
metaphysics like the proof of the existence of God,
the notion of substance, and the identity of the
self, he retained the Cogito in its revised empiricist form as the highest metaphysical principle,
nay, as the *only* speculative principle from which
all our knowledge must be deduced. Hume does not
bother even to say like Descartes or Locke that
everyone knows by himself what perception is, he
starts by asserting that everyone knows the distinction between the two kinds of perceptions:
impression or feeling and idea. He also assumes
that nobody would take perceptions to be corporeal.

However, even a hundred years or more after the Galilean revolution in physics and Descartes' onslaught
on scholasticism, Hume felt that Descartes' ambitious
positivistic plan as expressed in Part VI of the
Discourse was endangered, especially in the realm of
the moral sciences, by some contradictions inherent
in the Cartesian way of ideas. The contradictions
were not so much in the doctrine of ideas itself as

in the attempts to explain with ideas the interaction between body and mind as a species of causal
relation. To this effect and in order to obviate
these difficulties Hume accepted the changes made
by Locke and Berkeley in the doctrine of ideas.
The basic principle of physics, the distinction
between mind and body, is retained by Hume in the
doctrine as the ultimate principle of speculative
thinking; but, at the operative level, Descartes'
Rule is strictly observed—in the sense that ideas
are endowed with properties which make them the
sole ingredients in our knowledge both logically
and metaphysically. Because of these inherent
characteristics perceptions can be distinguished
from each other, and impressions can be distinguished
from ideas. Hume translates the basic distinction
between body and mind from the speculative scientific level to the operative level and he could
do this translation only because human sentiments
and ideas had been endowed by Descartes' rhetorical
innovation with the capacity to be the criteria of
objectivity. No psychological analysis *per se* can
reveal to us what is meant by distinctness of ideas
in the Cartesian or Humean sense if the speculative
scientific dimension of ideas is overlooked.

But the passage from the speculative level to the
operative level was dictated to Hume by his conviction that the whole thrust of the language of
ideas will be jeopardized if the problem of the
origin of our ideas will remain one of the problems
to be solved by Moral Philosophy. Thus, although
later in the *Treatise* Hume will say that perceptions
may be caused and are indeed caused by motion and
matter, in the opening section he writes that the
impressions of sensation are produced by unknown
causes or describes impressions as entering, without
specifying how, into the mind. It is only in the
section dealing with the immateriality of the soul
in Part VI of the *Treatise*, after analysing the idea
of necessary connexion and of causality, and after
summing up the tenets of Modern Philosophy that
Hume deals with the problem of interaction between
body and mind. By then causality will have been
explained in terms exluding any occult power.

Bearing in mind our comparison between the structure
of Descartes' First Meditation and the structure of
Section XII of the *Enquiry* "Of the Academical or
Sceptical philosophy" (see Chapter II), we have to
examine the reasons why Hume calls his philosophy
a sceptical or academical philosophy of mitigated
scepticism. The essence of the Cartesian notion
of the understanding is an understanding which
never goes beyond what is strictly within its possibilities of providing explanations for all phenomena. It is, for instance, to provide over and
above what is required in a scientific explanation
of gravity to suppose the falling stone to be endowed with knowledge of the centre of the earth.
It is equally to go beyond the requirements of the
understanding to explain what is doubt by something
more than an existing thinking mind. In a word, the
limitation of the understanding is not based so
much on something to be deplored in our fallen state
but on the recognition that our understanding can
distinguish between what is clear and what is obscure
and ununderstandable. In a sense, the Cartesians,
reject all the scholastic entities, substantial
forms, sensible and intellectual species, and others,
on the ground that these entities make knowledge
impossible when every one knows from common experience that we do distinguish the true from the false
and thus do know certain things for sure. Scholasticism limits the understanding in the sense of
systematically curtailing our confidence in our
capacity to know. The Cartesian limitation of the
understanding is a safeguard against error, since
it is an error to invoke occult and secret powers
in the explanations of natural phenomena.

The success of Cartesian philosophy was due among
other things to its explanation of the paradigm
error of scholastic philosophy. The error was due
to the propensity of the mind to go beyond the limits
of the understanding. The understanding is not
fallacious although it is limited. Besides, seen
as a whole, the new way of exploring nature was
based on a total scepticism concerning our childhood habits of interpreting nature in terms of our
sentiments. The methodic doubt is a surrogate, lest

we forget, used by Descartes in the First Meditation
for the principles of the new physics. So not only
did Hume formulate his philosophy in the language
of ideas, but he also assumed that the scepticism
on which Modern Philosophy is based, and the doctrine of ideas were simply two sides of the same
coin. Scepticism, in general, according to Hume
is always parasitic on the various philosophical
attempts to explain and overcome the doubts concerning our intellectual capacities. But, so Hume
thought, when scepticism is built into the philosophy itself, that is when we are left with nothing
to be certain about except our ideas, consequent
scepticism or parasitic scepticism is left without
any axe to grind.

However, Hume was aware that even Modern Philosophy
supplying as it did modern science with its most
successful speculative principle - the doctrine of
ideas - contained still some obscure notions which
did not fail to arouse the interest of consequent
sceptics. Among these obscure notions the most
important was the notion of power as distinct from
the exercise of power. Hume was even confident
that once philosophy gets rid of this notion, other
obscure notions like that of substance will become
superfluous. Hume does not begin his analysis of
the concept of cause from the scholastic conception. In both his books on science and on philosophy Descartes had already stressed the importance
of reducing the four kinds of causes to one only:
the efficient cause. Besides, in his Reply to the
First Objections, he defends his proof for the existence of God by his new concept of causality which
does not distinguish between the essence of the
cause preceding its effect and the exercise of causality. In Cartesian philosophy, the notion of an
efficient cause distinct from its effect and existing
as efficient cause before producing its effect, and
even if it has no occasion to produce it, is unthinkable. It is true that in the *Meditations* and the
Replies to the Objections, Descartes' decisive argument against the scholastic notion of cause is
sometimes overlooked because these arguments are
put forward, *en passant*, in order to show that God

causes himself since anyhow a cause cannot exist
qua cause prior to its effect. Even if in exploring
cause in the natural world we are restricted to
those causes which are prior in time to their effects,
this does not mean that we cannot envisage a limiting case, as in the case of God causing himself
into being, where the cause is simultaneous with its
effect:

> "Finally, I have not said that it is impossible
> for anything to be its own efficient cause; for
> although that statement is manifestly true when
> the meaning of efficient cause is restricted to
> those causes that are prior in time to their
> effects or different from them, yet it does not
> seem necessary to confine the term to this mean-
> ing in the present investigation. In the first
> place the question would in such case be unmean-
> ing, for who does not know that the same thing
> can neither be prior to nor different from it-
> self? Secondly, the light of nature does not
> require that the notion of an efficient cause
> should compel it to be prior to its effects;
> on the contrary, a thing does not properly con-
> form to the notion of cause except during the
> time that it produces its effect, and hence is
> not prior to it." (HR II 13-14).

Descartes does not innovate here; many thinkers,
Hobbes for instance also discarded the division of
causes into four kinds, and yet Descartes was successful in clarifying the notion of the causal relation as the concomitancy of cause and effect. The
principle of efficient cause, even if causality still
retains its rational character, becomes: *no causality
unless there is concomitancy of cause and effect*. But
of course from this formulation of the principle
of causality to the awareness that something
has been lost in our natural conception of
causes there is but an easy step. This step, together with how to remedy for the loss, was taken
by Malebranche who rejected the view that causality
is mere sequence and made God the sole and universal
cause. This explained the origin of our ideas,
bypassed the difficulty in the notion of interaction
between two distinct substances, mind and body, and

reduced natural causation to occasional causes.

However, logically speaking, other conclusions could
be drawn from the comcomitancy theory of causality.
As we mentioned it in Chapter II, Joseph Glanvill,
a champion of the Royal Society, a crusading anti-
Aristotalian, an admirer of Descartes, drew from
the notion of causality as nothing but concomitancy
the conclusion that not every event must have a
natural cause, it can also have a supernatural cause.
Glanvill held the view that witches and spirits
could be accounted for by scientific methods of
testimony and accused of dogmatism those unbelievers
who denied that witches existed. Glanvill's views
are consistently held together. In his book *The
Vanity of Dogmatizing* he founded his arguments against
dogmatism on the weakness of our understanding, a
weakness which is illustrated by our ignorance about
our intellectual powers. The interaction between
mind and body is, according to Glanvill, clouded
with mystery, and the representative power of sensation is inexplicable; before the Fall, *Adam*

> "needed no Spectacles. The acuteness of his
> natural Opticks (if conjecture may have credit)
> shew'd him much of the Coelestial magnificence
> and bravery without a *Galilaeo's* tube... (5).

After the Fall all our faculties are impaired and
we do not understand how we know nor do we see the
secret wheels of nature. That we do not see but
concomitancy in a causal relation is not attributed
by Glanvill to the fact that there is nothing to be
seen but to the fact that we cannot see the power
which is causality. If we cannot see the causal link
or power, it might well be the case that the causal
relation is only one of the probable explanations of
a phenomenon. And in his posthumous book *Saducismus
Triumphatus* edited by his friend Henry More, Glanvill
first showed how logically there might be witches and
then, on the basis of testimonies of reliable
witnesses, he showed that witches do exist.

In a long note to Section 57 of the *Enquiry* Hume
reveals to us that some form of Malebranchian theory

of causality was prevalent among what he calls
'modern metaphysicians':

> "Des Cartes insinuated that doctrine of the uni-
> versal and sole efficacy of the Deity, without
> insisting on it. Malebranche and other Cartesians
> made it the foundation of all their philosophy.
> It had, however, no authority in England. Locke,
> Clarke, and Cudworth, never so much as take
> notice of it, but suppose all along, that matter
> has a real, though subordinate and derived power.
> By what means has it become so prevalent among
> our modern metaphysicians?" (E 73).

And naturally Hume saw in all these theories about
the real location of the causal power the fertile
soil on which scepticism and superstition thrive.
If the theory of necessary causes was in difficulty
in the realm of nature then it was useless to try
to argue that the Doctrine of necessity prevails
also in the mental and moral realm. Norman Kemp
Smith may or may not be right in his hypothesis
that most of the Book of Morals was written by Hume
before the other two Books or at least before Book
I *On the Understanding*. What is much more plausible
is that Hume wrote the *Treatise* because he wanted
to vindicate the view that history, politics, morals,
criticism would have no foundations whatsoever were
it not for the fact that men do adhere in all their
thinking and practice to the doctrine of necessity:

> "Nor have philosophers ever entertained a diff-
> erent opinion from the people in this particular.
> For, not to mention that almost every action of
> their life supposes that opinion, there are even
> few of the speculative parts of learning to which
> it is not essential....It seems almost impossible,
> therefore, to engage either in science or action
> of any kind without acknowledging the doctrine
> of necessity, and this *inference* from motive to
> voluntary action, from characters to conduct."
> (E 89-90).

And in Section 72 of the *Enquiry* he gives us the rat-
ionale of all his method by showing that the doctrine
of necessity holds for nature and man alike whether

in physical, moral or mental matters. Instead of
going directly to the problem of liberty and necessity and start solving the problem by examining the
faculties of the soul, the influence of the understanding, and the operations of the will, he advises
us to

"first discuss a more simple question, namely,
the operations of body and of brute unintelligent
matter; and try whether they can there form any
idea of causation and necessity, except that of
a constant conjunction of objects, and subsequent
inference of the mind from one to another. If
these circumstances form in reality, the whole
of that necessity, which we conceive in matter,
and if these circumstances be also acknowledged
to take place in the operations of the mind, the
dispute is at an end; at least, must be owned to
be thenceforth merely verbal." (E 93).

In short, Hume applies the Cartesian Rule of ideas
to the problem of causation in nature; and, when
he thinks that he has solved the problem not only
in terms of ideas but also in the spirit of the
basic speculative principle of Natural philosophy,
he feels that he has grounded the notion of necessity as far as possible. Hume's theory of the
nature of the causal relation is the outcome of the
development of the doctrine of ideas (which says
that qualites are not in the objects but perceptions
in the mind) to its logical conclusion. Just as
modern science could not develop without stopping
man's inclination to project his feelings onto
objects, so also moral philosophy could not start
without first stopping man from projecting onto the
objects that feeling of necessity which depends on
an inference in the mind. It is only when we cease
thinking that we have an idea of necessity and
causation in the operations of the external objects
over and above the idea of constant conjunction and
the subsequent inference in the mind, that we can
accept the idea that the same necessity and the
same causation obtain in mental and moral matters.

Hume applies to the problem of causation the same

method Descartes applied to the problems concerning
the nature of mind or the nature of the magnet.
The error to be avoided in all these cases is to
go further in our answers than what is required by
our understanding. It is because metaphysicians
have supposed that in their answer to the question
about the nature of causation or necessity they
must include some unknown power, some secret agency,
that they have arrived at the conclusion that God
is the final cause, or that natural causes are not
the only powers operating in the universe, or finally that causes are not all necessary causes:

> "But philosophers, observing that, almost in
> every part of nature there is contained a vast
> variety of springs and principles, which are hid,
> by reason of minuteness or remoteness, find that
> it is at least possible the contrariety of events
> may not proceed from any contingency in the cause,
> but from the secret operation of contrary causes."

The vulgar may attribute the uncertainty of events
to the *contingency of causes*, while the scientist is
certain that contrariety of effects always betrays
contrariety of causes. And from this they conclude

> "that the connexion beween all causes and effects
> is equally necessary, and that its seeming uncer-
> tainty in some instances proceeds from the secret
> opposition of contrary causes." (E 86-87).

Hume's central thesis is that all causes are necessary causes, and that there is no idea of contingency whatsoever in the notion of causality.
Necessity Hume defines conformably to the definitions
of cause since anyhow necessity is an essential
part of causality. It consists either in constant
conjunction of like objects, or in the inference of
the understanding from one object to another, and
Hume adds that both these definitions are at bottom
the same.

Bearing in mind that Hume regards Modern Philosophy
as stemming form an absolute sceptical attitude to
our childhood habits and to scholastic philosophy,

it is no wonder that he calls his answer to the
sceptical doubts concerning the operations of the
understanding, the sceptical solutions of these
doubts. Hume is always aware of the fact that the
doctrine of ideas (which entails that all the problems of the understanding must be solved in terms
of ideas and of relations of ideas), is also a topic
of absolute scepticism; hence his reduction of
causation to the idea of the conjuction of two
objects and to the subsequent inference in the mind
is called by him a sceptical solution. It is therefore impossible to advance the view that Hume could
have reached his conclusion about causation without
what many call the psychologistic terminology of ideas.
Working as he was within the Cartesian system of
ideas which embodies the speculative principle of
the new concept of scientific objectivity, he could
not develop these principles and apply them to the
analysis of the ideas of causation and of necessary
connexion without using a doctrine which he never
questions: the doctrine of ideas. It is to mis-
conceive the cardinal importance of the rhetorical
innovation of Descartes, an innovation which allowed
the spread of Cartesianism in England, to consider
the terminology of ideas as subjectivistic and to
imagine that Hume could have reached his views about
causality independently of the Cartesian Rule of
Ideas.

On the other hand, it is of the greatest importance
to distinguish carefully between what Hume calls
a sceptical solution, and what most historians call
a sceptical conclusion, when we are examining the
Humean theory of causation. Hume meant his solution
to put an end to the doubts about men's capacity to
look for causes and to the doubts about the necessity of causes. These doubts Hume attributed to the
human propensity to go beyond the limit of our understanding and hence all these doubts are really unfounded. Hume uses the same argument Descartes
uses in the *Regulae* when he shows that the simple
natures are known *per se* and are wholly free from
falsity. We may imagine ourselves to be ignorant
of things like causation and necessary connexion,
but in fact we are not. And our error consists in

looking for something over and above what is present to our understanding, viz. constant conjuction
of objects and an inference in the mind. When we
know this, our doubts concerning our capacity to
discover causes and necessary connexions vanish.
Nevertheless we must not overlook the principles
from which we started to arrive at such a positive
conclusion concerning causality. The principles
are those discovered in physics and imply the rejection of the notion that qualities are in the
objects since in fact they are perceptions in the
mind. These principles are in direct opposition to
all our other natural beliefs in the existence of
external objects; hence these principles are essentially sceptical beliefs and any solution we reach
with their help is a sceptical solution.

However, we cannot ignore Hume's insistence on the
fact that causal inference has no foundation in
reason and his further distinction between demonstrative reasoning and matter of fact reasoning.
This aspect of Hume's theory of causation has led
many historians, if not all of them, to conclude that
Hume's scepticism consists merely in his assertion
that causal reasoning is not demonstrative. But
such a conclusion overlooks completely the import
of Hume's argument showing that matter of fact
reasoning is not demonstrative. The whole point
of denying that induction is not deduction (in our
uses of the terms) is to allow Hume to offer a
positive theory of causality as an answer to all the
post-Cartesians theories which end, according to
Hume, in transforming causality into a mysterious,
occult, unitelligible power, and which open the
door to all sorts of superstitions and beliefs in
supernatural powers:

> "'Twill only be proper, before we leave this sub-
> ject, to draw some corrollaries from it, by which
> we may remove several prejudices and popular errors,
> that have very much prevail'd in philosophy.
> First, We may learn from the foregoing doctrine,
> that all causes are of the same kind, and that
> in particular there is no foundation for that
> distinction, which we sometimes make betwixt
> efficient causes, and causes *sine qua non;* or be-

twixt efficient causes, and formal, and material,
and exemplary, and final causes.... For the same
reason we must reject the distinction betwixt
cause and *occasion*, when suppos'd to signify any
thing essentially different from each other. If
constant conjunction be imply'd in what we call
occasion, 'tis a real cause. If not, 'tis no
relation at all, and cannot give rise to any
argument or reasoning. Secondly, The same course
of reasoning will make us conclude, that there is
but one kind of *necessity*, as there is but one kind
of cause, and that the common distinction betwixt
moral and *physical* necessity is without any foundation in nature.... As objects must either be
conjoin'd or not, and as the mind must either
be determin'd or not to pass from one object to
another, 'tis impossible to admit of any medium
betwixt chance and an absolute necessity....
The distinction, which we often make betwixt
power and the *exercise* of it, is equally without
foundation." (T 171)

If causality were a species of rational connexion
as Descartes probably assumed and Locke vaguely
hinted, the whole project of Descartes and the
Cartesians to transform Knowledge into an on - going
process from the known to the unknown would be
thwarted. In such a case we would be able to iden-
tify a cause independently of the actual prod-
uction of its effect and even without the occasion
of producing the effect. We could thus by demonstrative reasoning not only prove the possible
existence of existent objects but also their actual
existence. But had this been really the case,
Descartes would not have needed in the *Meditations*
anything besides the assurance that his mathematical
reasoning is valid: he could have passed from its
validity to its capacity to prove the existence of
the external world. But Descartes did at this
juncture need again yet another proof of the Exis-
tenc of a non-deceiver God and only then could he
assent to the veracity of his faculties in informing
him about the actual existence of external objects:

"Nothing further now remains but to inquire

whether the material things exist. And certainly
I at least know that these may exist in so far
as they are considered as the objects of pure
mathematics, since in this respect I perceive
them clearly and distinctly." (HR I 105)

So the state in which Descartes left our possibility
to know that external objects exist was quite clear
and Hume drew the necessary conclusion. In all the
operations of the understanding we are always proceeding from the known to the unknown:

"In the disquisitions of the understanding, from
known circumstances and relations, we infer some
new and unknown." (E 290).

Given the basic principle of objective scientific
thinking that qualities are not in the object put
perceptions in the mind, knowledge would not be
knowledge if its object is not something concealed,
and unknown. In Descartes the guarantee that our
faculties are not fallacious is the existence of
a non-deceiver God, in Hume the guarantee of our
true beliefs is in the determination of nature to
make us feel, reason and believe. In both cases
a guarantee is required and yet neither Descartes
nor Hume seem to deplore in the least this so-called
gap between mind and objects. On the contrary, what
is for modern epistemologists a gap is for the Cartesian a redefinition of knowledge: all previous
notions of knowledge which construed the objects in
terms of sentiment or construed knowledge itself
as some presence of the objects in the mind are
considered false and an explanation of why they
are false is given in terms of the distinction between mind and body.

This being the case, nothing could be more fallacious than the comparison between Russell's doubts
about induction and Hume's sceptical solution of his
doubts about the nature of the causal relation. It
is usually assumed that Hume's theory of causation
implied that we seem not to know whether the laws
of nature which we establish by inductive reasoning are the right ones and that we cannot secure

ourselves against the eventuality of a change in
the secret springs of nature. The example given
by Russell in *The Problems of Philosophy* about the
chickens which for five hundred days have been fed,
expect the same the following day and yet are killed
instead, illustrates vividly Russell's basic approach to the difference between induction and deduction. Russell deplores the fact that induction,
which is according to him the method of science,
is not as secure as deduction which is the method
of logic and mathematics.[2] But, as we have pointed
out before, Hume evolves the new modern notion of
induction, quite distinct from both the Aristotelian
and the Baconian notions, as the logical outcome of
the struggle of Cartesianism against the scholastic
notions of occult hidden powers. To leave the causal
relation to be as rational as a mathematical relation
would mean to leave the notion of experience totally
inarticulate and to revert to verbal disputations
as conducive to knowledge.

It is true that Hume in a sense deplores that
induction is not as secure as demonstration, but
he would have deplored much more a notion of cause
or power which by definition the understanding could
never grasp. The same discovery which is seen by
Hume as a victory for science, is seen by Russell as
a shortcoming of the foundations of human knowledge.
The two philosophers are indeed talking about the
same logical distinction between induction and deduction but in totally different contexts. In the
case of Hume the distinction is the result of the
articulation of the vague conception of knowledge
as identified with logic. In the case of Russell
the distinction is the starting point of multiple
attempts by his followers to try, if not to cancel
the distinction, at least to attenuate its drastic
character.

There is a further important difference between the
modern approach to the problem of induction and
Hume's analysis of the nature of the idea of necessary connexion. It is not only the case, as we
have shown, that Hume developed the Cartesian Rule
of Ideas and applied it to the knowledge of causes,

he also developed in his own way the principle of
distinction in order to distinguish not only mind
from body but also action from speculation. What
has been called the Copy Principle, that every idea
is a copy of a preceding impression, is not only
an epistemological principle or a criterion of
meaning or even an empirical generalization. It
is also a significant addition to the Cartesian
principles of speculative thinking: Hume wants to
extend speculative thinking to the realm of action.
Thinking is done with ideas, action is linked with
passion and feeling:

> "Every one of himself will perceive the difference
> betwixt feeling and thinking"

writes Hume in the opening section of the *Treatise*,
but in the *Enquiry* he begins the same section entitled "Of the Origin of Ideas" with a more forcible
statement:

> "EVERY one will readily allow, that there is a
> considerable difference between the perceptions
> of the mind, when a man feels the pain of exces-
> sive heat, or the pleasure of moderate warmth,
> and when he afterwards recalls to his memory
> this sensation, or anticipates it by his imag-
> ination. These faculties may mimic or copy the
> perception of the senses; but they never can
> entirely reach the force and vivacity of the
> original sentiment." (E 17).

Thus the reduction of necessity to a feeling in the
mind has a double aim: on the one hand the causal
link is nothing more than what is present to the
understanding, on the other hand, causal inference
becomes on the level of action an acquired habit,
as determined by nature as natural instincts:

> "I shall add, for a further confirmation of the
> foregoing theory, that, as this operation of the
> mind, by which we infer like effects from like
> causes, and *vice versa*, is so essential to the
> subsistence of all human creatures, it is not
> probable, that it could be trusted to the fall-
> acious deductions of our reason, which is slow

in its operations; appears not, in any degree,
during the first years of infancy; and at best
is, in every age and period of human life, extre-
mely liable to error and mistake. It is more
conformable to the ordinary wisdom of nature to
secure so necessary an act of the mind by some
instinct or mechanical tendency, which may be
infallible in its operations, may discover itself
at the first appearance of life and thought, and
may be independent of all the laboured deductions
of the understanding". (E 55)

What appears to some metaphysicians, contemporaries
of Hume, as a negative description of the causal
relation, when it is reduced to concomitancy, is
viewed by him as a positive characteristic. If
causality was more than concomitancy we could infer
the secret power of bread to nourish us from the
first appearance of its sensible qualities without
the aid of experience; but this is contrary to the
findings of modern science, argues Hume, and con-
fuses experience with demonstrative reasoning. If
the actual occasion of the inference of the mind
had to be preceded by the perception of the necessary
link between cause and effect, our beliefs would
never move us to action. What in our days is deplored in Hume's theory of causality as nothing but
mere uniformity and a subjective feeling of expec-
tation, is considered by Hume as a step forward towards an objective view of the world, and how the
latter is parallelled by the emotive nature of our
causally determined beliefs. The term, impression,
which is introduced by Hume in philosophy is not
just a new name for sensation, sentiment, feeling,
emotion, or passion. He calls them by this new
name because he needs the new term in his speculations about thinking and action. The new term is
indispensable for understanding Hume's philosophy
in general and as the development of Descartes'
ideas in particular.

For Descartes the certainty of the Cogito, if we
recall his reduction of all perceptions to passions,
is the knowledge of the necessary existence of a
felt idea. Bearing in mind that this self-awareness

of one's feelings assumed the basic distinction between mind and body and hence embodied the first
principle of knowledge, it is understandable that
a philosopher like Hume who wants to extend philosophical speculations to actions, would try to
isolate the element of necessity, of existence, and
of feeling, in the Cartesian notion of Idea.

The distinction of the various elements in ideas
is not limited to the contrast between feeling and
thought. Existence for instance is implied in the
impression or feeling and not in the ideas. An
idea can convey the notion of existence if it is
either enlivened by the impression which is its
proper cause or if it is associated with another
impression. An idea as such can only convey the
notion of possible existence. Real existence and
matter of fact cannot be inferred without the presence of an impression or a feeling. It might well
be the case that Hume's elaboration of the Cartesian
notion of idea is nothing but a return to Descartes'
initial conception of human feelings as signified
by natural signs. In the first chapter of *Le Monde
ou Traité de la Lumière* Descartes compares the human
sentiments to linguistic signs, which are conven-
tional, arbitrary, having no resemblance whatsoever to the things they refer to:

"Vous savez bien que les paroles, n'ayant aucune
ressemblance avec les choses qu'elles signifient,
ne laissent pas de nous les faire concevoir, et
souvent même sans que nous prenions garde au son
des mots, ni à leurs syllabes; en sorte qu'il
peut arriver qu'après avoir ouï un discours, dont
nous aurons fort bien compris le sens, nous ne
pourrons pas dire en quelle langue il aura été
prononcé. Or, si des mots, qui ne signifient
rien que par l'institution des hommes, suffisent
pour nous faire concevoir les choses avec
lesquelles ils n'ont aucune ressemblance, pourquoi
la Nature ne pourra-t-elle pas aussi avoir établi
certain signe, qui nous fasse avoir le sentiment
de la lumière, bien que ce signe n'ait rien en
soi qui soit semblable à ce sentiment? Et n'est-
ce pas ainsi qu'elle a établi les ris et les
larmes, pour nous faire lire la joie et la

tristesse sur le visage des hommes?" (Alquié I
315-316)

The language of ideas derives its objectivity primarily from the new science and its rejection of any
animistic or anthropomorphic interpretations of
nature, but it needed also to be construed as a
language of the natural signs. It is true that in
the above passage, the sign is the physical action
and the signified is the human sentiment, but later
in the *Meditations* the sensations will become the
signs for what is useful and agreeable. Whatever
the interpretation of the function of the sentiment,
whether as sign or as signified, it is important to
stress the arbitrary character of the relation between the significant and the signified. Unlike
language, the language of ideas is determined by
nature, though both of them are totally dissimilar
to what they signify. In a sense, there are in the
doctrine of ideas two presuppositions about language:
the first, that the relation ideas-objects is
arbitrary as the relation between linguistic signs
and the conceptions they invoke in the human mind;
the second, that while linguistic signs are convent-
ional, ideas are caused and determined by nature
or God.

It might be the case that many misinterpretations
of Hume's philosophy stem not so much from how we
understand what he means by "idea" as from how we
construe what he means by "impression". More often
than not "impression" is taken to be just another
word for image, and Hume's insistence on the importance of feelings in the explanation of human
actions and hence of the importance he attributed
to the distinction between impression and idea is
overlooked. Whenever Hume is dealing with beliefs,
existence, the existence of objects, the nature of
moral distinctions, in short whenever he needed to
speculate on the prerequisites of action, Hume uses
the term, "impression", and not the term "idea".
Thus to take one example, the belief in the existence of external objects is analysed in terms of
impressions, i.e., how we attribute to our impressions
a continued and distinct existence. We do not con-

sult reason or rely on philosophical principles in
order to reach such a conclusion. And, if we do
insist on trying to explain the origin of this belief, then the only way to link into one object
the successive but interrupted ideas we have had in
the past is in terms of a propulsion arising out of
the "lively impressions of the memory": a propulsion
which bestows a vivacity to what is, to all intents
and purposes, a product of the imagination, and
transforms it into a belief. As the principle of
human actions must be instituted by nature, it must
be explained in terms of feelings or impressions and
not ideas. Nature has left us no choice and we must
assent to the principle concerning the existence of
body. Ultimately the principle guiding our daily
practice is always a manner of feeling. We cannot
subsist if we do not believe in the existence of
bodies and equally we would perish if we do not
believe our inferences of like effects from like
causes. Yet there is a direct opposition between
the two beliefs:

> "'Tis this principle, which makes us reason from
> causes and effects; and, 'tis the same principle,
> which convinces us of the continu'd existence
> of external objects, when absent from the senses.
> But tho' these two operations are equally natural
> and necessary in the human mind, yet in some cir-
> cumstances they are directly contrary, nor is it
> possible for us to reason justly and regularly
> from causes and effects, and at the same time
> believe the continu'd existence of matter."
> (T 266)

However, even if the two beliefs are not the product
of reason, yet the assumptions of the belief in the
external existence of objects are directly contrary
to the assumptions of the causal inference:

> "When we reason from cause and effect, we con-
> clude that neither colour, sound, taste, nor smell
> have a continu'd and independent existence. When
> we exclude these sensible qualities there remains
> nothing in the universe, which has such an exis-
> tence." (T 231)

This means that philosophical speculation leading to
the doctrine of ideas, as we have been repeatedly
warned, is not meant for day to day practice: it
does not mean anything to a painter that colour is
not in the object but only a sensation. When we are
hearing, seeing, feeling, loving, hating, desiring,
willing, in short, when we are actually engaged in
life we cannot but be guided by our impressions
which lead us to believe in the existence of objects;
but when we are thinking we are guided by our ideas
which ultimately lead us to deny existence to any
thing but our ideas. To reflect on our causal reasoning leads us to ideas, while to reflect on our
actions leads us to impressions. Impressions are
introduced by Hume when he begins his development of
Cartesianism so as to include not only the nature of
knowledge but also the motives for action; and since
nothing can be the motive for action except a feeling
he had to separate the feeling from the idea in the
Cartesian notion of a felt idea.

Another misconception of the Humean analysis of causation arises from the difference between our use of
the expression, matter of fact, and his use. Hume
usually takes matters of fact as results of inferences and not of observation. Here again, it would
be wrong to assume that Hume's conception of facts
is the same as ours. The very notion of fact as
that of induction is the result of the Cartesian
way of philosophising. Matter of fact, as we read
in the Oxford Dictionary, is opposed in the time
of Descartes and Hume to matter of law. A matter of
fact is the way one argues to prove that the alleged
facts are true and this way of arguing is contrasted
with an argument whether the law is relevant or not
to the case in question. In our use of the term,
fact, it is assumed that facts are not in need of
any proof, facts are what our sense impressions directly inform us about. Hume is aware that both our
senses and our causal reasoning lead us to construct
reality:

    "Of these impressions or ideas of the memory we
    form a kind of system, comprehending whatever we
    remember to have been present, either to our

internal perceptions or senses; and every particular of that system join'd, to the present
impressions, we are pleased to call a *reality*.
But the mind stops not here. For finding, that
with this system of perceptions, there is another
connected by custom, or if you will, by the relation of cause or effect, it proceeds to the con-
sideration of their ideas; and as it feels that,
'tis in a manner necessarily determin'd to view
these particular ideas, and that the custom or
relation, by which it is determin'd, admits not
of the least change, it forms them into a new
system, which it likewise dignifies with the
title of *realities*. The first of these systems
is the object of the memory and senses; the second
of the judgment." (T 108)

Matters of fact were not deemed to be argued for by
causal reasoning only. Testimony could also, independently of any reasoning, prove a matter of fact.
This explains the inclusion of the *Essay on Miracles*
in the *Enquiry* as Section X "Of Miracles". In this
section Hume argues that testimony is not a method
of proof because it is based on the principle of
the veracity of witnesses and the veracity of the
senses, but because it is a species of causal reasoning. When testimony is thus construed, its use
for proving the occurrence of miracles could be assessed by the principle of apportioning one's belief
to evidence. By this he means that if one is led by
two distinct matter of fact reasonings to two contrary beliefs one should choose that belief for which
one has more evidence. In the particular case of a
reported miracle, even if the testimony is reliable
as causal reasoning, we cannot accept its verdict
because it contradicts the whole system of the laws
of nature based also on matter of fact reasoning.
Thus an event would not be called a miracle if it
happens in the common course of nature.

All alleged facts are brought by Hume under the scru-
tiny of matter of fact reasoning. Once we no longer
rashly suppose that we have some further idea of
necessity and causation in the operations of the
external objects than the experience of constant

conjunction and the inference in the mind, we no
longer look for something more in the explanation of
the voluntary actions of the mind. In the way that
a body can move another body so also a motive can
produce an action of the body. We do not need an
unintelligible doctrine of liberty to explain the
relation between thought and action. Similarly,
though there appears no connexion between motion
and thought, the case is the same as that of all
causes and effects. We do not need the unintelligible
notion of substance, let alone of two distinct substances, in order to explain the cause of our perceptions:

> "If you pretend, therefore, to prove *a priori*, that
> such a position of bodies can never cause a thought;
> because turn it which way you will, 'tis nothing
> but a position of bodies; you must by the same
> course of reasoning conclude, that it can never
> produce motion; since there is no more apparent
> connexion in the one case than in the other. But
> as this latter conclusion is contrary to evident
> experience, and as 'tis possible we may have a
> like experience in the operations of the mind,
> and may perceive a constant conjunction of thought
> and motion; you reason too hastily, when from the
> mere considerations of the ideas, you conclude
> that 'tis impossible motion can ever produce
> thought, or a different position of parts give
> rise to a different passion or reflexion." (T 247-
> 248)

Hume's advice consists in leaving aside the problem
of the substance of the mind and the even more
mysterious problem of the union of soul and body
and confining ourselves to the problem of the cause
of thought. If we do so,

> "We find by comparing their ideas, that thought
> and motion are different from each other, and by
> experience, that they are constantly united;
> which being all the circumstances, that enter
> into the idea of cause and effect, when apply'd
> to the operations of matter, we may certainly
> conclude, that motion may be, and actually is,
> the cause of thought and perception." (T 248)

When the mystery is taken out of the notion of causal necessity and we no longer suppose that there is something over and above what is within the reach of the understanding in the causal relation, the latter can be used to solve all the difficulties inherent in the notion of substance, and in the distinction and union of substances. Just as we explain how a body can move another body we can explain how mind can affect body and body affect mind. The Cartesian dualism which is essential for the new concept of scientific objectivity is maintained by Hume by his original development of the Cartesian way of ideas so as to apply to the idea of necessary connexion. We can now reformulate the new Doctrine. Instead of: qualities are not in the objects they are perceptions in the mind we must say with Hume: qualities and powers are not in the objects they are perceptions in the mind. Could one still maintain that Hume's analysis of causation is a sceptical conclusion?

1.   Norman Kemp Smith, *The Philosophy of David Hume*, London, 1941.

2.   Bertrand Russell, *The Problems of Philosophy*, Williams & Norgate, London and Holt, New York, 1912.

CHAPTER VI
Humean Ethics

We have tried to distinguish in the preceding chapter what Hume calls "a sceptical solution" of the
nature of the causal relation from what many commentators have called "a sceptical conclusion" of Hume's
speculation about the origin of the idea of necessary
connexion. We face a similar problem in the present
chapter: can we show that Humean ethics based on the
principle that moral distinctions are not derived
either from reason or matter of fact, is not conducive to scepticism in moral matters? If any thing
which is neither mathematics nor science is metaphysics and hence not worthy of any rational philosophical speculation, how can we avoid the obvious
conclusion that morality which is based neither on
relation of ideas nor on causal reasoning, is therefore utterly subjective and doubtful? Though it is
usual for commentators to take both Hume's arguments
concerning matter of fact reasoning and concerning
moral distinctions in order to characterise his
Pyrrhonian sceptical outlook, it is evident that
such a characterisation is based on a misleading
analysis of the arguments and a further misleading
conclusion concerning Hume's outlook.

It is important at first to stress the difference,
in regard to reason, between the status of causal
reasoning and that of moral distincions: while the
first is still included albeit in a very diluted
form in the province of rationality, of thinking,
the latter is absolutely outside reasoning and thinking. This being said, Hume's view of causality as
well as his view of morality is part of the application of the experimental method to moral philosophy. Thus matter of fact reasoning and moral
distinctions are both related (through the experimental method) and contrasted (through the opposition between reason and feeling).

143

Besides, if the doctrine of ideas is interpreted as
it is usually done, that is, as the misapplication of
introspective psychological methods to philosophical
problems, Hume's distinction between reason and sentiment, between ideas and impressions, appears to
be totally devoid of any crucial consequence. What
does it matter to distinguish between idea and impression if both are "private" perceptions and as
such unsuitable as the basis for an objective outlook in any intellectual discipline?

It is only if we retrace the origin of the doctrine
of ideas to the Cartesian reflections on what constitutes scientific and objective speculation, that
we can understand the use of ideas and impressions
in Hume's philosophy. In general, it would help us
to understand Hume's moral philosophy to remember
that all Cartesians start from the assumption that
the condition for reaching any objectivity in our
speculations is to distinguish categoricaly between
moral matters, i.e. between logical, moral and critical matters on the one hand and physical matters
on the other.

Hume, let us recall it again, mentions the doctrine
of ideas both in the *Treatise* and in his essay "The
Sceptic", when he states his view that morality
and art are based on feeling. Just as we can reason
about objects even though qualities are perceptions
in the mind and not in the objects, so we can distinguish between the just and the unjust even though
the feeling of approbation is not in the action.
When the understanding is operating with ideas there
seems to be always a real, though often unknown standard in the nature of things, while when taste is
operating with sentiments or impressions, no less
real a standard is assumed, not in the nature of
actions or things but in the structure of the mind.
Both in our logical and our moral activities there
are standards and these standards guarantee the
reality of our judgments and of our moral distinctions:

"Those who have denied the reality of moral distinctions, may be ranked among the disingenuous

disputants; nor is it conceivable, that any human
creature could ever seriously believe, that all
characters and actions were alike entitled to the
affection and regard of everyone. The difference,
which nature has placed between one man and another, is so wide, and this difference is still
so much farther widened, by education, example,
and habit, that, where the opposite extremes come
at once under our apprehension, there is no
scepticism so scrupulous, and scarce any assurance so determined, as absolutely to deny any
distinction between them." (E 169-170)

It is very difficult to gather from the first two
Books of the *Treatise* what Hume was aiming at and
even more difficult to see their relevance to the
third Book *Of Morals*. Hume recognises the difficulty
and attributes it to the abstruse character of his
speculations concerning the understanding and the
passions. The opening paragraph of Book III is
strikingly similar to Descartes' revelations to the
authors of the Sixth Objections, about how he was
not persuaded in spite of the logical and metaphysical demonstrations of the distinction between mind
and body:

"There is an inconvenience which attends all
abstruse reasoning, that it may silence, without
convincing an antagonist, and requires the same
intense study to make us sensible of its force,
that was at first requisite for its invention.
When we leave our closet, and engage in the common affairs of life, its conclusions seem to
vanish, like the phantoms of the night on the
appearance of the morning; and 'tis difficult
for us to retain even that conviction, which we
have attain'd with difficulty". (T 455)

Nevertheless, Hume is hopeful that his philosophical
conclusions which he has reached so far as the Understanding and the Passions are concerned, will be
corroborated by their application to morals. *An
Enquiry concerning Human Understanding* is more helpful
if one wants to put in a summary form the philosophical principles which Hume wants to apply to the

principles of morals. What makes the *Enquiry* more
helpful than the *Treatise* is the fact that from all
Book II *Of the Passions* Hume decided to choose the
section "Of Liberty and Necessity" and included it in
the first *Enquiry*. On the basis of this inclusion,
one could venture to assert that Hume's conclusions,
before starting his speculation on ethics, consisted
in the principle that there is but one kind of cause,
the necessary causes, and in the doctrine of necessity which applies to both the physical and the mental world and to their relation:

> "And indeed, when we consider how aptly *natural*
> and *moral* evidence link together, and form only
> one chain of argument, we shall make no scruple
> to allow that they are of the same nature, and
> derived of the same principles." (E 90)

Incidentally, this passage appeared also before,
in the Treatise, with one substantial difference:
there, Hume uses the term "cement" instead of the
term "link". Now we are in a position to grasp
Hume's intention when in the penultimate paragraph
of the first *Enquiry* he tells us how far morals and
criticism can be the object of reasoning and enquiry,
i.e. how far he can extend to morals and criticism
his conception of what is reasoning:

> "Morals and criticism are not so properly objects
> of the understanding as of taste and sentiment.
> Beauty, whether moral or natural, is felt, more
> properly than perceived. Or if we reason con-
> cerning it, and endeavour to fix its standard,
> we regard a new fact, to wit, the general tastes
> of mankind, or some such fact, which may be the
> object of reasoning and enquiry." (E 165)

Thus Hume's intention is first to show that taste
is distinguishable from the understanding and then
to show by matter fact reasoning which actions and
characters are the subject of moral approbation.
In a sense the first part of his moral speculations
is the extension of the Cartesian principle of never
to assume in the object of the enquiry something
over and above what is stricly necessary and understandable, and the second part of his speculation

is the extension of his conception of causal reasoning to generalise about attributes of the mind
which render a man an object either of esteem and
affection, or of hatred and contempt. As a matter
of fact the second part of Hume's intention is more
largely elaborated than the first, and sometimes he
gives the impression that provided no one is going
to confuse moral distinctions with matter of fact
or demonstrative reasoning, his main task is to
find by matter of fact reasoning the general characteristic of commendable actions.

"The only object of reasoning is to discover the
circumstances on both sides, which are common
to these qualities; estimable and blameable
qualities ; to observe that particular in which
estimable qualities agree on the one hand, and
the blameable on the other; and thence to reach
the foundation of ethics, and find those universal principles, from which all censure and approbation is ultimately derived. As this is a
question of fact, not of abstract science, we
can only expect success, by following the experimental method, and deducing general maxims from
a comparison of particular instances." (E 174)

If he invokes the doctrine of ideas and recalls its
success in the philosophy of nature when he defends
the view that moral distinctions are a matter of
feeling and not of reason, he equally recalls the
success of the experimental method in its application to natural philosophy when he defends the view
that it is by matter of fact reasoning that we can
discover the universal principles from which all
censure or approbation is ultimately derived.

However, if we articulate the doctrine of ideas in
relation to the doctrine of necessity and how Hume
working within the former proves the latter, and
then return and corroborate the first by arguing
with the help of the second, it becomes clear that
the experimental method has two aspects and sometimes Hume uses the one and sometimes the other.
Besides, when he deduces by the experimental method
the general maxims from a comparison of particular

instances, he immediately reverts to the principle
that moral distinctions are felt rather than judged;
he asserts that these maxims would not be appealing
by themselves and that it is only because we have in
us the sentiment of humanity that we recognise these
causal conclusions, these maxims, as moral maxims:

> "We may observe, that all the circumstances re-
> quisite for its operation are found in most of
> the virtues; which have, for the most part, a
> tendency to the good of society, or to that of
> the person possess'd of them. If we compare all
> these circumstances, we shall not doubt, that
> sympathy is the chief source of moral distinctions;
> especially when we reflect, that no objection can
> be rais'd against this hypothesis in one case,
> which will not extend to all cases. Justice is
> certainly approv'd of for no other reason than
> because it has a tendency to the public good:
> And the public good is indifferent to us, except
> so far as sympathy interests us in it." (T 618)

The two sets of arguments Hume deploys for elabora-
ting his system of morals could also be contrasted
as one set of positive arguments showing by observation and generalisation that the good of mankind
is the only object of morality, and another set of
negative arguments showing that precepts, laws, and
regulations, have nothing to commend them to human
approval or disapproval. These negative and positive arguments could be contrasted also as inductive and deductive (in our sense of inductive and
deductive). And when we remember the general tendency to equate philosophical arguments with logical arguments, we can understand the contemporary
tendency to isolate the negative or deductive set
of arguments as the most important issue in Humean
ethics. There is however some form of over-simpli-
fication to see Hume's negative arguments as similar
to modern arguments contrasting value judgments with
factual judgements. For, if the latter is a real
dichotomy, the value judgement becomes essentially
non-propositional. But while Hume seems to say many
things about the moral judgment which would fit with
the view that moral judgments are non-propositional,
many other things which Hume says do not fit at all.

In may be very useful to remember that when Hume
reaches the stage of dealing with morality, he has
already shown that society is founded on necessary
principles in the context of his arguments for a
uniform kind of necessity holding for physical and
moral matters alike:

> "We must certainly allow, that the cohesion of
> the parts of matter arises from natural and nec-
> essary principles, whatever difficulty we may find
> in explaining them: And for a like reason we must
> allow, that human society is founded on like prin-
> ciples; and our reason in the latter case, is
> better even that in the former; because we not
> only observe, that men *always* seek society, but
> can also explain the principles, on which this
> universal propensity is founded." (T 401-402)

This universal propensity, Hume describes as a gradual development from the necessity of different sexes
to copulate, through parenthood care, to close union
and confederacy of adults. Nevertheless, Hume is
aware that the propensity to unite is sometimes ser-
ved by laws and precepts which have nothing to do
with the interest and happiness of human society.
If we compare superstitious regulations with the rules
of justice we cannot see in them *qua rules* anything
to distinguish one from the other. The necessity of
justice for the support of society does not reside
in the law itself or in the relation between the
different parts of the law. Nor does the necessity
lie in the action recommended by the law or in the
relation which obtains between various actions recommended by the law. It is only the usefulness of
the law for the public good which is the criterion
for commending or condemning a particular law:

> "But there is this material difference between *super-
> stition* and *justice,* that the former is frivolous,
> useless, and burdensome; the latter is absolutely
> requisite to the well-being of mankind and exis-
> tence of society. When we abstract from this
> circumstance (for it is too apparent ever to be
> overlooked) it must be confessed, that all regards
> to right and property, seem entirely without found-
> ation, as much as the grossest and most vulgar
> superstition." (E 199).

It is not very difficult to observe the similarity between Hume's arguments concerning the idea of necessary connexion and his arguments about the characteristic of justice as the necessary support of society. In both cases, neither the idea of necessary connexion, nor the idea of justice as necessary to society is really an idea: the idea of necessary connexion is the felt inference in the mind, while the necessity of justice for the existence of society is perceived by our feeling of approbation. Besides, both the idea of justice and that of necessary connexion are derived from experience, they are not of an instinctive origin, they are not innate ideas:

> "All birds of the same species in every age and country, built their nests alike: In this we see the force of instinct. Men in different times and places, frame their houses differently: Here we perceive the influence of reason and custom. A like inference may be drawn from comparing the instinct of generation and the institution of property." (E 202)

The institution of property presupposes the idea of justice which is a human invention based on experience. We can understand Hume's insistence that the standard of justice is not an *a priori* principle discovered by a kind of mysterious intuition: a priorism may ground the necessity of justice in an absolute standard but in reality it ends in an absolute scepticism, since both superstition and justice could be claimed to be intuited, as indeed they are claimed. The insistence of metaphysicians that causality cannot be only concomitance of two events is, as we have shown in the preceding chapter, an insistence which leads to a consequent scepticism. It is only by a systematic doubt about a priorism that we can reach an idea of necessity as founding all our scientific activities about the physical as well as the moral world. We cannot argue against a metaphysician who insists on not accepting causality as constant conjunction. Our solution of our doubts concerning causality cannot be anything except a sceptical solution.

The same argument applies to the institution of justice.
We cannot decide on what is necessary for the existence of society except by comparing the ends of
superstition and justice. The question is why did
not Hume conclude that the idea of justice is a belief caused in us by the comparison of ends? In other
words, why did Hume not conclude that moral distinctions are a species of matter of fact reasoning?
Does he not from a series of descriptive statements
about superstition and a further series of descrip-
tions of justice reach the conclusion that the latter
is absolutely requisite to the well-being of mankind
and existence of society?

Before answering this question we must consider how
Hume argues that the actions recommended by superstition and by justice could not be distinguished
when we restrict our examination to the actions only:

> "Those who ridicule vulgar superstitions, and
> expose the folly of particular regards to meats,
> days, places, postures, apparel, have an easy
> task; while they consider all the qualities and
> relations of the objects, and discover no adequate
> cause for that affection or antipathy, veneration
> or horror, which have so mighty an influence over
> a considerable part of mankind. A Syrian would
> have starved rather than taste pigeon; an Egyp-
> tian would not have approached bacon: But if these
> species of food be examined by the senses of sight,
> smell, or taste, or scrutinized by the sciences
> of chemistry, medicine, or physics, no difference
> is ever found between them and any other species,
> nor can that precise circumstance be pitched on,
> which may afford a just foundation for the reli-
> gious passion." (E 198)

Such reflections which could be made in the same manner about the sentiments of justice are, according
to Hume, very obvious in the case of superstitious
practices and if these prevail it is not by mistake
or by ignorance but owing to education, prejudice and
passion. However, if Hume is trying to argue that it
is by the effects of the laws or of the actions recommended by the laws that we judge these laws or these

actions, it certainly does not mean that these effects are not factual. If one compares the useful
and the useless it cannot be the case that what makes
them what they are is not something which could not
by definition be grasped by our understanding. A
hint is given, however, by Hume why ultimate ends of
human actions, can never, in any case, be accounted
for by reason but recommend themselves entirely to
the sentiments and affections of mankind without any
dependence on the intellectual faculties:

> "Ask a man *why he uses exercise;* he will answer, *because
> he desires to keep his health.* If you then enquire,
> *why he desires health,* he will readily reply, *because
> sickness is painful.* If you push your enquiries far-
> ther, and desire a reason *why he hates pain,* it is
> impossible he can ever give any. This is the ulti-
> mate end, and is never referred to any other ob-
> ject.
>
> Perhaps to your second question, *why he desires health,*
> he may also reply, that *it is necessary for the exercise
> of his calling.* If you ask, *why he is anxious on that
> head,* he will answer, *because he desires to get money.*
> If you demand *Why? It is the instrument of pleasure,* says
> he. And beyond this it is an absurdity to ask for
> a reason. It is impossible there can be a progress
> *in infinitum;* and that one thing can always be a rea-
> son why another is desired. Something must be
> desirable on its own account, and because of its
> immediate accord or agreement with human sentiment
> and affection. (E 293)

And since, adds Hume, virtue is desirable on its own
account, without fee or reward, merely for the immed-
iate satisfaction which it conveys; it is necessary
that some human sentiment which distinguishes between
good and evil is touched by the appearance of virtue.
In the above argument the moral sense theory of ethics
is given a Cartesian formulation which reminds us of
how Descartes in the *Regulae* argues that the simple
natures must be known *per se,* otherwise we cannot
explain our power to distinguish the true from the
false. There Descartes was arguing that the error
in Scholastic philosophy was to suppose that there
is something over and above what is given to the

understanding such as "real qualities," and substantial forms, and when these unknowable entities are
assumed our capacity to distinguish the true from
the false is itself in doubt. Hume, similarly maintains that since we can always ask on and on for a
further reason why a thing is desired we could not
make moral distinctions, as we are all aware that
we do, were it not the case that there is something
which is desired on its own account. This argument
of Hume is certainly much more powerful, logically
speaking, than his negative arguments against the
possibility of moral distinctions being made by the
understanding whether by demonstrative or matter of
fact reasoning. Unlike the argument based on in-
finite regress, those used by Hume in the opening
section of Book III draw their power of persuasion
mainly from particular examples and illustrations.

What Hume calls the impossibility that "there can be
a progress *in infinitum!*" is an argument which could
throw some light on the notion of introspective certainty, or as Descartes calls it, internal testimony.
In *The Search after Truth,* Descartes speaking through
Eudoxus, says that all our efforts to define what
white is are in vain, while in order to know it it
is only requisite to open one's eyes and see the
white. In the case of definition of what white is,
just as in the case of the reason why to avoid pain
our enquiries end by seeing white and by feeling
hatred for pain. The realm of internal testimony is
the realm of those certainties which if questioned
would make insecure all our knowledge and our taste.
The indubitability of our sentiments is not based
so much on the *special capacity to look inward into ourselves,* and see what is white or feel a sentiment of
approbation towards virtue, as it is based on the
argument that the real possibility of knowledge which
we do have, and the no less real possibility that we
have to distinguish between good and evil, require
that something be *known without the possibility of defining
it,* and something be *desirable per se without further reason whatsoever.* In a way when we say that moral distinctions presuppose the existence of an end for
which no reason can be given besides being approved
for its own sake, we clarify the real intention of

Hume when he argues against the view that virtue is
nothing but a conformity to reason.

When the negative arguments Hume uses in the opening
section of the *Treatise* are formulated in a positive
form in order to show that moral distinctions are made
by feeling and not by reason, it is very difficult to
see any connection between them and the arguments of
modern moral philosophers asserting the dichotomy value-
fact. Hume seems however to confirm sometimes the view
that moral judgments cannot be true or false as descriptive factual judgments can be:

> "Reason is the discovery of truth or falshood.
> Truth or falshood consists in an agreement or
> disagreement either to the *real* relations of
> ideas, or to *real* existence and matter of fact.
> Whatever, therefore, is not susceptible of this
> agreement or disagreement, is incapable of being
> true or false, and can never be an object of our
> reason. Now'tis evident our passions, volitions,
> and actions, are not susceptible of any such agree-
> ment or disagreement; being original facts and
> realities, compleat in themselves, and implying
> no reference to other passions, volitions, and
> actions. 'Tis impossible, therefore, they can
> be pronounced either true or false, and be either
> contrary or conformable to reason." (T 458)

We have, in the preceding chapter, stressed the fundamental difference between the way Hume uses the expression "matter of fact" and ours. In the above
passage he goes further and insists that where there
is no discovery there are no matters of fact. Hume
would not call the information he has by a present
impression a matter of fact. This is the reason why
he distinguishes between the system formed by impressions and ideas of memory and the system formed by
cause and effect. In the first there is no unknown,
everything is present in the mind with no reference
to other impressions. In the second there is always
an unknown idea to which we refer and which we discover by our customory inference. Hume, in Appendix
I of the *Enquiry Concerning the Principles of Morals,* con-

trasting reason with taste writes:

> "From the circumstances and relations, known or
> supposed, the former leads to the discovery of
> the concealed and unknown; after all the circum-
> stances and relations are laid before us, the
> latter makes us feel from the whole a new senti-
> ment of blame or approbation." (E 294)

We should not hasten and conclude that far from distinguishing value from fact as some contemporary
moral philosophers do, Hume takes moral distinctions
to be factual in our sense of the word, to be some
non-inferred truths, although he does not use the
term "factual" as we do, and would refuse to call an
impression true or false.

It is obvious that our difficulties in interpreting
Hume's philosophy in general and his moral philosophy
in particular are due to a basic difference between
Hume's conceptual framework and ours. To say that
Hume was one of the precursors of the emotivist theory of ethics is to gloss over a fundamental discre-
pancy between Hume's use of the term "sentiment" and
ours. While an emotivist holding that moral sentences are not propositions which could be true or
false usually infers that these sentences lack the
objectivity he attributes to factual propositions,
Hume, on the contrary, holds that moral distinctions
are as real as any conclusions from relation of ideas
or matter of fact reasoning. In the same Appendix I
Hume writes about the standard of reason and the
standard of taste:

> "The standard of the one, being founded in the
> nature of things, is eternal and inflexible, even
> by the will of the Supreme Being; the standard of
> the other, arising from the eternal frame and con-
> stitution of animals, is ultimately derived from
> that Supreme Will, which bestowed on each being its
> peculiar nature, and arranged the several classes
> and orders of existence." (E 294)

Hume, unlike modern emotivists, starts from the assumption that we do make moral distinctions between

good and evil, virtue and vice and hence his arguments unlike theirs are not aimed at settling the
question whether moral arguments have or have not
any standard of objectivity. Hume starts from the
real possibility of making moral distinctions, while
emotivists start from a sceptical attitude whether
moral distinctions are at all possible; Hume saw that
beyond the variety of moral principles there was necessarily one moral standard, universal and permanent:

> "The notions of morals implies some sentiment
> common to all mankind, which recommends the same
> object to general approbation, and makes every
> man, or most men, agree in the same opinion or
> decision concerning it. It also implies some
> sentiment, so universal and comprehensive as to
> extend to all mankind, and render the actions and
> conduct, even of the persons the most remote, an
> object of applause or censure, according as they
> agree or disagree with that rule of right which
> is established." (E 272)

The moral sentiment is not an internal rule, a kind
of mental yardstick by which we judge the moral
value of actions and of characters. Since the rule
of right is not innate, then it must be determined
by examining the moral relations of actions, which
in their turn, are determined by the comparison of
actions to rules. And this of course is obviously
reasoning in a circle. Hume on the other hand starts
by defining virtue as whatever mental action or quality gives to a spectator the pleasing sentiment of
approbation. And this feeling, not to be confused
with non-moral pleasure, exists in every individual
however weak that feeling might be:

> "Let these generous sentiments be supposed ever
> so weak, let them be insufficient to move even
> a hand or finger of our body, they must still
> direct the determinations of our mind, and where
> everything else is equal, produce a cool preference
> of what is useful and serviceable to mankind,
> above what is pernicious and dangerous." (E 271)

So, since every man has this feeling of approbation,
the philosopher proceeds to examine what actions have

such an influence on the mind. The result of Hume's
experimental reasoning when applied to explain the
rules of property is that the moral sentiment cannot
be a kind of instinct, otherwise we would need for
that purpose a multitude of instincts to be applied
to cases of the greatest intricacy:

> "For when a definition of *property* is required,
> that relation is found to resolve itself into any
> possession acquired by occupation, by industry,
> by prescription, by inheritance, by contract, &c.
> Can we think that nature, by any original instinct,
> instructs us in all these methods of acquisition?"
> (E 201-202)

Other institutions and practices, such as inheritance
and contract, are necessary to determine property,
not to speak of judges, praetors, chancellors and
juries. Should we include all these in the definition of property? The answer of Hume is that there
is a one-one relation between the sentiment of humanity which is the same in all men and the idea of justice which consists of its usefulness to society.
Property is then defined as one of the rules of justice.

We shall not insist again, as we did in the preceding
chapter, on the importance of the distinction between
impression and idea in Hume's development of Cartesianism from the speculations about the understanding to speculations about action. Ideas explain
reasoning and impressions explain action. There is,
however, an important distinction to be made between
an impression of pleasure and pain and an impression
of moral pleasure or moral distress. The former can
guide us in our actions and reactions to objects and
men, while the latter can guide us in our actions
and reactions to men in society only. That is why
Hume describes the feeling of approbation when the
action is considered as a whole, as a new feeling.
Describing taste in Appendix I Hume writes that it

> "has a productive faculty, and gilding or staining
> all natural objects with the colours, borrowed
> from internal sentiment, raises in a manner a new
> creation." (E 294)

This new creation, the feeling of approbation, is not
derived from nature but from artifice and yet the
new feeling is not contrary to our natural passions,
otherwise it could not be efficacious in restraining
what is heedless and impetuous in them. Thus it would
be impossible to construe Hume's theory of morals as
saying that moral distinctions are about human feelings, about events and occurrences in the mind. We
can gauge the difficulty we experience in understanding Hume by the kind of misleading interpretation
given by Reid of the view that the perception of
beauty is merely a feeling in the mind:

> "If it be said that the perception of beauty is
> merely a feeling in the mind that perceives, with-
> out any belief of excellence in the object, the
> necessary consequence of this opinion is, that
> when I say Virgil's Georgics is a beautiful poem,
> I mean not to say any thing of the poem, but only
> something concerning myself and my feelings. Why
> should I use language that expresses the contrary
> of what I mean?" (*Essays* 759)

Reid as usual is writing after the Cartesian revolution has succeeded in distinguishing our intellectual
faculties from their objects. He takes for granted
that objects as such are not a constitutive part of
knowledge. Hume, on the contrary, belongs to the
Cartesian revolution; he is consolidating its results
and expanding its conquests to the realm of action,
morality, and criticism. For him a feeling is never
just a feeling, a fact about the mind. Its main
characteristic is its being distinct from the object
it surveys or feels. The self-referential property
of sentiments, feelings, and ideas is not the limitation Reid deplores in the doctrine of ideas in general and in the theory of taste in particular but is
for Hume as for Descartes the reflection of the distinctness between thought and object. We can think
and feel objects provided we do not assume that our
thought and feeling are in the objects. Reid is
wrong when he thinks that Hume's theory of criticism
implies that we do not say anything about a poem when
we say that it is beautiful but only something about
ourselves and our feelings. On the contrary, taste
goes further than the understanding:

s not the same with the qualities
leformed, desirable and odious, as
falsehood. In the former case, the
tent with merely surveying its
/ stand in themselves: it also
it of delight or uneasiness, app-
ie, consequent to that survey; and
letermines it to affix the epithet,
2d, desirable or odious." (*Essays* 166-

e same essay, "The Sceptic", why
at the agreeable feeling of app-
e object. We do not believe that
ngeance are separable properties
e of themselves, we know that they
from the structure of the passions
esire such pursuits, and yet with
virtue we suppose that the case
igreeable quality is thought to
ind not in the sentiment which
int and as violent as other human
:inguishable easily from the ob-
jeet. It is important to notice that this is the
standard paradigm example given by all the Cartesian
holders of the doctrine of ideas which is nothing but
the generalisation from "pain is not in the object"
through "heat is not in the flame" to "qualities are
not in the objects but perceptions in the mind".
Instead of "pain" Hume uses "vengeance" and instead
of sensible qualities he talks about beauty as an
agreeable quality. But in no case does Hume forget
or overlook the connexion between the feeling of
approbation and the nature of the object. The feeling of approbation cannot occur if we are still ignorant about the nature of the object, i.e. if we have
not already surveyed the objects as they are.

Reid is much nearer to us when he calls moral and
esthetic distinctions moral and esthetic judgments.
Sometimes Hume also calls morals distinctions, judgements:

"The mind can never exert itself in any action,
which we may not comprehend under the name *percep-*

tion; and consequently that term is no less appli-
cable to those judgments, by which we distinguish
moral good and evil, than to every other operation
of the mind. To approve of one character, to condemn another, are only so many different perceptions." (T 456)

But more often than not he wants to distinguish
sharply between moral judgments and others and hence
he opts for the term "distinction" for affirmations
in the realm of morality. In his distinction between
'is' and 'ought' he says that 'ought' expresses some
new relation or affirmation. One of the reasons for
his new usage is that he wanted to reserve the term
'judgment' for the conclusions of causal reasoning.
A judge's verdict is a judgement because among other
things he must either accept or reject the proof
or disproof of the *alleged facts*. The judge does not
know yet if the facts will or will not be proved,
they are still unknown. It is only when all the unknown elements have been solved that the judge can
decide if the acts are lawful or unlawful. Unlike
a factual judgement which Hume calls speculative
proposition or affirmation, he calls a moral distinction a decision or affirmation.

It is evident by now that it would be a most unre-
warding task to try to provide a lexicon for the
translation of Humean concepts into ours. The reason
being that while part of what Hume says is perfectly
understandable, another part is ununderstandable because it was meant as an antidote to a whole way of
thinking, knowing, and feeling. The old way of thinking and feeling was essentially based on a world of
objects which were not indifferent to human feelings.
It must have been the case that Hume thought that
the new way of seeing the world, an indifferent world
of alien particles moving around and devoid of any
human sentiment, would not be protected against the
encroachments of anthropomorphic and animistic ways
of knowing and feeling the world - without interpreting the world of art and morality in terms of the
Cartesian doctrine of ideas.

colour which becomes an idea of red or the idea of
pain which is the copy or effect of the impression
of pain. Is the expression "idea of justice" a mis-
nomer? Obviously not, since when Hume is speculating
about the origin of justice he is not feeling in his
bosom the sense of common interest, and besides he
repeatedly reminds the reader that one can know what
justice is without acting in accordance with the
rules of justice: *virtue is certainly not knowledge.*

But there is still a difference between impressions
of colours and the general sense of common interest:
the first gives rise to ideas and then to beliefs
about the external world, the second constitutes our
decisions to act in society. But since belief is
also more of an emotive than of a cognitive nature,
all our actions are ultimately divorced from speculations, and in the end it seems that we can distinguish the functions of the impression of pain, the
impression of red, and the sentiment of approbation,
by our different levels of experience. No experience
is needed to act on feeling pain. The impression of
red is not sufficient by itself to lead us to action,
we need to relate the impression of red to other
perceptions in order to make the impression relevant
to our actions. The feeling for justice leads directly to action and yet it presupposes a great deal
of experience. It is similar to the feeling of pain
in its being an ultimate justification for itself
and yet the pain we feel when contemplating an unjust
act is not the cause of our moral condemnation. We
feel pain because we condemn. As for the experience
we need before being capable of making moral distinctions, Hume distinguishes such an experience from
that needed for evolving our knowledge of the external world by saying that the first results in an
invention, a convention, while the second results
in a discovery. An invention is a new way of feeling
ushering us into a mode of behaviour which is the
product of the artifice of man. Such a new behaviour
could lead us to believe that the world has changed,
that we have discovered new relations between actions
and things, when in fact it is only we who have
changed. The Cartesian injunction never to return
to the scholastic way of manufacturing the world

with our own perceptions is strictly applied to the
realm of morality and criticism: justice and beauty
are not qualities of the objects they are perceptions
in the mind. The difficulty of extending Cartesianism
to morals and criticism lies in the fact that these
two modes of activity are creative in a sense that
science is not and hence we tend easily to project
on the outside world new creations and take what are
really changes in ourselves as discoveries in things
we approve or condemn.

Could we say that philosophy or more strictly moral
philosophy which includes logic, morals, and criticism is also an activity which depends on experience
for its development and which consists in a new way
of seeing the world? Are the terms "impression",
"idea", "necessary connexions" as used by Hume linguistic, rhetorical inventions which express his new
way of seeing the world?

CONCLUSION
Conceptual Continuity
or Conceptual Revolution

There is a general conception which dominates modern
accounts of philosophy: the conception that philosophical problems are best illustrated by pointing
out the different levels of reality to which belong
language on the one hand, and the external world
about which we talk in language on the other. The
difference in these levels, no matter how we construe
it, is always seen as *a gap* and we naturally interpret all past philosophies as attempts to deal with
this gap. We tend to think that Hume, following
Descartes, has sharpened our awareness concerning the
possibility (or rather impossibility) of justifying
our knowledge of the external world in terms of the
subjective evidence available to us.

We have tried to show that the Cartesian philosophical project was scientific and realistic and that
Descartes never doubted the possibility of knowledge.
The basic principle of the distinction between mind
and body was indispensable in order to avoid the main
error of the scholastics: that all our knowledge
is uncertain because there are things or qualities
which are unknowable in principle. Since for the
scholastics there was no distinction between mind and
body, they were led to attribute "real qualities" or
"occult qualities" to things.

In order to justify his rejection of these unknowable
qualities, Descartes will evolve a notion of the
understanding as the locus of the criteria which help
us to distinguish between what is knowable and what
is "over and above" our capacity to know. Descartes
did not start by declaring that the nature of knowledge is problematic: on the contrary, he starts by
showing that for the scholastics knowledge is
problematic because their scepticism is simply an
error, and what is more, an error of their own
fabrication.

Similarly, in ethics, Hume never questioned the reality
of moral distinctions. His speculations on moral
matters meant to show that those who proclaimed the
demonstrative nature of moral reasoning ended up in
absolute relativism because they anchored their
moral distinctions in arbitrary choices unfounded in
human nature or matter of fact reasoning.

We must therefore conclude that what we see as a "gap"
between thought and reality and which we attribute
to Cartesian dualism was a conceptual innovation of
Descartes. This innovation was made in order to put
an end to a theory of knowledge implying some identity
between the object and the knowing mind. The doctrine
of ideas constituted the best guarantee against the
projection of human sentiments on the external world.

Descartes certainly and Hume also (although sometimes
equivocally) admitted that their theory of mind was a
piece of speculative metaphysics or "true metaphysics"
as Hume called it. We have tried to show that the
gist of this speculative metaphysics was ultimately
a matter of conceptual innovation: in the new use
of the term "idea" and in the new use of the term
"cause". Such a linguistic reform was needed to
familiarise the readers with the new methods of
physics, with science, in contrast to the pseudo-
science of the scholastics and the ensuing
scepticism.

The analytic approach to the history of philosophy has
a natural tendency to study past philosophy in terms
of conceptual continuity. This tendency is usual in
history *qua* history. By reducing revolution to a
covert continuation of past tradition, history tends
to explain revolutions away. On the other hand,
conceptual analysis ignores the conditions in which
the philosophy in question has emerged and concentrates
solely on the arguments of the text. Unfort-
unately, the assessment of past arguments is made
in the light of paradigmatic arguments of the day,
and any shift in the meaning of terms is overlooked.

There is a world of difference between say Descartes'
or Hume's defence of science with the help of their

metaphysical speculations and Russell's rejection of
speculative metaphysics in favour of the scientific
attitide. The method of Cartesianism makes the
solution of *scientific problems* possible by defining the
limit of speculative metaphysics so as to exclude
what is over and above the understanding from the
domain of scientific knowledge. Russell's method of
logical analysis makes the resolution of *philosophical
problems* possible by defining the limits of scientific
philosophy so as to exclude speculative metaphysics.

It would be helpful to articulate the difference in
terms of the so-called "gap" between thought and
reality. In the case of the Cartesians the "gap" is
voluntarily adopted for the sake of scientific
objectivity. In Russell's case we have to recall
how the "gap" in the form of the dreaded dichotomy
between appearance and reality was exploited by
Russell's predecessors like Bradley, in order to
advance the view that scientific knowledge is a
distorted knowledge and that only philosophy or rather
philosophical arguments can deal with the philosophical problem of the "gap". Russell does not deny that
there is a philosophical problem of the "gap" between
appearance and reality. He admits its existence and
deplores it implicitly in his phenomenalism and in
his doubts about induction. But he also tries with
the help of logical analysis to account for our knowledge of the external world in terms of an individual's "private world", i.e. the class of all the
data within that individual's perspective.

It is obvious that for the Cartesians it is
philosophy which comes to the help of the new physics
by evolving a new metaphysics, or rather a new
doctrine of what is knowledge. In the case of
analytic philosophy, it is philosophy which is in
need of help. In the 17th and 18th centuries what is
at stake is *science;* in our century what is at stake
is *philosophy* which is riddled with problems--or
rather with pseudo-problems.

Lately there seems to be a growing awareness among
modern authors about the doubtful character of some
perennial problems of philosophy. But this awareness

has not yet reached the stage when philosophy itself can be viewed as an activity, involving the use of language as a signifying activity, and creating its ontological commitment.

Bibliography

1. Arnauld, Antoine et Pierre Nicole. *La Logique ou l'Art de Penser*. Introd. Louis Marin. Flammarion, Paris, 1970.

2. Brissenden, R. F., ed. *Studies in the Eighteenth Century*. Australian National Univ. Press, Canberra, 1968.

3. Descartes. *The Philosophical Works of Descartes*. 2 vols. Ed. Haldane, Elisabeth S. and G. R. T. Ross, Cambridge Univ. Press, 1911-12, 1934.

4. Descartes. *Oeuvres Philosophiques*. 3 tomes. Ed. Ferdinand Alquié. Garnier Frères, Paris, 1963-1973.

5. Gilson, Etienne. *Discours de la Méthode: Texte et Commentaire*. Cinquième edition. Paris, J. Vrin, 1976.

6. Gilson, Etienne. *Etudes sur le rôle de la pensée médiévale dans la formation du système cartésien*. Paris, J. Vrin, 1951.

7. Glanvill, Joseph. *The Vanity of Dogmatizing: The Three 'Versions'* by Joseph Glanvill. Introd. Stephen Medcalf. Harvester Press, Hove, Sussex, 1970.

8. Glanvill, Joseph. *Saducismus Triumphatus*. London, 1689. Introd. Coleman O. Parsons. Gainesville, Florida, 1966.

9. Gouhier, Henri. *La pensée métaphysique de Descartes*. Paris, J. Vrin, 1962.

10. Hume, David. *A Treatise of Human Nature*. Ed. L. A. Selby-Bigge. Oxford Univ. Press, Oxford, 1888, 1968.

11. Hume, David. *Enquiries Concerning the Human Understanding
    and Concerning the Principles of Morals*. Ed. L. A. Selby-
    Bigge. Second Edition. Oxford Univ. Press, Oxford,
    1902, 1970.

12. Hume, David. *ESSAYS Moral Political and Literary*.
    Oxford Univ. Press, Oxford, 1963, 1974.

13. Hare, R. M. "Universalisability." *Proceedings of
    the Aristotelian Society*, LV (1954-55).

14. Kenny, Anthony. Review of *Descartes: The Project
    of Pure Enquiry* by Bernard Williams. *Times Higher
    Educational Supplement*, 14 August 1978.

15. Kemp Smith, Norman. *The Philosophy of David Hume*.
    London, 1941.

16. Lenoble, Robert. *Mersenne ou la naissance du mécanisme*.
    Paris, J. Vrin, 1943.

17. Locke, John. *An Essay Concerning Human Understanding*.
    2 vols. Ed. A. C. Fraser. Dover Publications,
    New York, 1959.

18. Mossner, E. C. *The Life of David Hume*. Nelson, 1954.

19. Macintyre, A. C. "Hume on 'Is' and 'Ought'."
    Hume: A Collection of Critical Essays. Ed. V. C.
    Chappell. Anchor Books, Doubleday, New York, 1966.

20. Noxon, James. *Hume's Philosophical Development: A
    Study of his Methods*. Clarendon Press, Oxford, 1973.

21. Popkin, Richard H. "Joseph Glanvill: A Precursor
    of Hume." *Journal of the History of Ideas*, XIV (1953).

22. Popkin, Richard H. "David Hume: His Pyrrhonism
    and His Critique of Pyrrhonism." *Hume: A Collection
    of Critical Essays*. Ed. V. C. Chappell. Anchor Books,
    Doubleday, New York, 1966.

23. Reid, Thomas. *Essays on the Intellectual Powers of Man*.
    Introd. Baruch A. Brody. MIT Press, 1969.

24. Ryle, Gilbert. *The Concept of Mind*, Hutchinson
    Univ. Library, London, 1949.

25. Rée, Jonathan. *Descartes*. Allen Lane, London, 1974.

26. Russell, Bertrand. *The Problems of Philosophy*.
     Williams & Norgate, London and Holt, New York,
     1912.

27. Sprat, Thomas, D.D. *The History of the Royal Society
     for the Improving of Natural Knowledge*. London, 1702.

28. Voltaire. *Letters Concerning the English Nation*.
     London, 1733.

29. Watson, Richard A. *The Downfall of Cartesianism
     1673-1712*. Martinus Nijhoff, The Hague, 1966.

30. Williams, Bernard. *Descartes: The Project of Pure
     Enquiry*. Penguin Books, 1978.

31. Wittgenstein, Ludwig. *Philosophical Investigations*.
     Trans. G. E. M. Anscombe. Second Edition.
     Blackwell, Oxford, 1968.

32. Wittgenstein, Ludwig. *The Blue and Brown Books*.
     Blackwell, Oxford, 1969.

Index of Names

Adam, 124
Aristotle, 22, 49, 59
Arnauld, 60, 77, 80,
    104, 119, 169

Bacon, 61
Berkeley, 23, 30, 42,
    49, 104, 119, 120
Bovary, Mme, 7
Brissenden, R. F., 94,
    116, 169

Caterus, 65, 66
Cicero, 62
Clarke, Samuel, 125
Columbus, 17
Copernicus, 29
Cudworth, R., 125

Dinet, Père, 70

Flaubert, 7

Galileo, 24, 29, 34, 55,
    84, 124
Gassendi, 29, 46, 66
Gibieuf, Père, 110, 113
Gilson, Étienne, 33, 34,
    35, 40, 46, 53, 57,
    65, 66, 80, 169
Glanvill, J., 21, 22,
    24, 26, 67, 72, 73,
    124, 169
Gouhier, H., 47, 57, 62,
    70, 169

Hare, R. H., 25, 170
Hobbes, 29, 66
Homais, 7

Jesuit, 1

Kant, 35
Kemp-Smith, N., 125, 141,
    170
Kenny, A. J. P., 56, 57,
    170
Kepler, 29

La Flèche, 1, 30
Launay, l'Abbé, 41
Leibniz, 30
Lenoble, R., 29, 57, 170
Locke, 23, 29, 31, 36, 49,
    72-74, 78, 80, 88, 104,
    119, 120-125, 170

MacIntyre, A. C., 15, 25,
    170
Malebranche, 23, 42, 104,
    119, 123, 125
Mersenne, 29, 66, 71
Mossner, E. C., 1, 25, 170

Noxon, J., 15, 25, 170
Nicole, P., 60, 77, 80,
    104, 169

Ovid, 6
Oxford Dictionary, 138